Cruising Speed
—A DOCUMENTARY

Cruising Speed

—A DOCUMENTARY

WILLIAM F. BUCKLEY, Jr.

G. P. Putnam's Sons
New York

TO GERTRUDE E. VOGT

with love and gratitude

BUCKLEY, William Frank, Jr., mag. editor, author; b. N.Y.C., Nov. 24, 1925; s. William Frank and Aloise (Steiner) B.; student U. Mexico, 1943; B.A., Yale, 1950; LL.D., St. Peter's Coll., 1969, Syracuse U., 1969, Ursinus Coll., 1969, Lehigh U., 1970, L.H.D., Seton Hall U., 1966, Niagara U., 1967, Mount St. Mary's Coll., 1969, D. Sc.O., Curry Coll., 1970; m. Patricia Taylor, July 6, 1950; 1 son, Christopher T. Asso. Editor American Mercury, 1952; editor-in-chief National Review, N.Y.C., 1955—; Syndicated column, 1962—; Host weekly TV show Firing Line, 1966—; Founder, Nat. Com. to Horsewhip Drew Pearson, 1967; U.S. Advisory Commission on Information, 1969—. Served to 2d lt., inf., AUS, 1944-46. Clubs: N.Y. Yacht, Overseas Press. (N.Y.C.); Nat. Press (Washington), Century. Recipient U. So. Calif. Distinguished Achievement Award in Journalism, 1968, Emmy Award for Outstanding Program Achievement, 1969. Author: God and Man at Yale, 1951; McCarthy and His Enemies (with L. Brent Bozell), 1954; Up From Liberalism, 1959; Rumbles Left and Right, 1963; The Unmaking of A Mayor, 1966; The Jeweler's Eye, 1968; The Governor Listeth, 1970. Editor: The Committee and Its Critics, 1962; Odyssey of A Friend, 1970; Did You Ever See A Dream Walking?, 1970. Contbr. Racing at Sea, 1959; The Intellectual, 1960; What is Conservatism?, 1964; Dialogues in Americanism, 1964; Violence in the Streets, 1968; The Beatles Book, 1968; Spectrum of Catholic Attitudes, 1969; Great Ideas Today, 1970; also periodicals. R.C., Republican. Office: 150 E. 35th St., New York City, N.Y. 10016.

MONDAY, NOVEMBER 30. The car pulls in at ten, and my wife, Pat, undertakes to supervise the loading of it. This is an operation, because it has been a long weekend, during which a lot of clutter accumulates that we'll need in New York, and there is the fruit and the cheese and the flowers that would spoil if we left them in Stamford until the weekend. Angela, the maid, will go with us; and our house guest Peter Glenville; and three dogs, *my* Rowley, and *her* Pepper and Foo, the last an ill-tempered, eccentric Pekingese, a gift from Marvin Liebman, one of the two or three people I would forgive the giving of a dog as a Christmas present; perhaps the only friend I would forgive the giving of Foo. I named horrible Foo, Foo, making the point firmly that to call him Fu would be in inexcusably bad taste. Pepper is a beautiful cavalier King Charles spaniel who loves Pat and naught else in this world, which I take unkindly. Rowley is also a cavalier, a Blenheim, quite simply the most beautiful, most engaging dog I ever saw, his only fault being that of Browning's Last Duchess, who smiled as sweetly for the gardener as for the Duke; in Rowley's case, he smiles even more sweetly for the gardener if there is any possibility at all that he is likelier than the duke to give him a) something to eat or b) a ride in the car, the two things Rowley cares most about, respectively, in all the world. Fortunately, he is quite stupid, so that it never fails that to keep him from jumping into the limousine and adding to the general chaos prematurely one has only to open the door to the Renault, as though that were the car we would be driving off in. Then you shut that door, while you calmly pack the Cadillac, and open it up only after you are ready for Rowley to join you.

11

I am waiting thirty yards down the driveway, opposite my garage-study, with my briefcases, and I squeeze in, and resume reading the research material for the two television shows that will be taped beginning at two-thirty: one of them with Jerris Leonard, who is the young Assistant Attorney General in charge of integrating the schools; the other with two Catholic college presidents, Father Kenneth Baker (S.J.) of Seattle University, and Sister Elizabeth McCormack (R.S.C.J.) of Manhattanville. There had already been a problem, transacted earlier this morning over the telephone. Sister Elizabeth did not want Manhattanville to be referred to as a "Catholic college." But, I said to the producer, Warren Steibel, that will hardly do, since the purpose of the television program is to bring together two college heads who are disagreed about the role that religion should play in the curriculum; Father Baker being outspokenly in favor of palpably-Catholic Catholic higher education, Sister Elizabeth believing something else—a decision that, the research suggests, she was perhaps necessarily driven to by the Blaine Amendment, which is a part of the Constitution of the State of New York and says that no state aid can go to a religious college. How does one cope with that, and qualify for the subventions available from the state to any nonreligious college—x number of dollars per degree granted? Why, unstress religion to the point of satisfying the educational authorities that yours is not a religious college in any meaningful sense. It comes to several hundred thousand dollars per year where Manhattanville is concerned, and for that much money, now-adays, you can just co-exist with a little cock-crowing. There is the second complication—that Father Baker,

12

having been in office for only a semester, has been eased out. Does that mean that his position on Catholic education has been officially repudiated? The point is, some things are personal, and we have to decide what to bring up during the program, and what we shouldn't bring up because it is of strictly personal, not public, concern. Call Sister Elizabeth, I had asked Aggie Schmidt—my colleague and researcher, and an ultramontanist graduate of Manhattanville—and tell her we are going to have to discuss the question of Manhattanville's Catholicism on the program, because after all that's the kind of thing the program is about; and if she wants to drop out, we'll go with Father Baker alone, if need be. The word comes back. Sister Elizabeth will take her chances.

We head out for New York. Pat and Peter chatter on, giggle, exclaim, while the dogs bound about, and I read the recent court decisions that have left so many people so confused about what the law demands, let alone the Constitution. I had written, earlier in the morning, the column I must write every Monday (and Wednesday, and Friday), and in it I thought to rebuke the House Committee on Un-American Activities, now called the Committee on Internal Security, for publishing the names of sixty-odd "radical" speakers who repeatedly appear on campus, and at the same time to rebuke the court that sought to restrain the committee from publishing its report. What the committee did, I thought and wrote (mostly, I write what I think, though not always, and sometimes I suppose I do not think enough before I write. Professor Paul Weiss at Yale used to say "I'm not as bright as my students; I have to think before I write"), was less mischievous than lazy. Better to find

13

out what the radicals are saying on the campuses than merely to brand them as such, and report that they are speaking on campus.

And there had been correspondence. Always there is correspondence. My former headmaster (Edward Pulling, of Millbrook School) demands to know what does "agenbite of inwit" mean—a phrase used by a professor at the University of Georgia who reviewed (favorably, which is why E. P. was sent the review) one of my books. I hadn't any idea, but didn't feel guilty about it, since Mr. Pulling didn't know and he is an English scholar; but obviously I had to find out, so Aggie called the professor. The phrase is Middle English, a translation of Friar Loren's *Somme*, more accurately rendered *Ayenbite of Inwit*, and meaning "remorse of conscience," and never mind the relevance of that to my book *The Governor Listeth* . . . An associate editor of *The Village Voice* had asked me a few weeks earlier to review a book, and I hovered over a decision, and then spotted the review in *VV* of Edward Banfield's *The Unheavenly City*, the operative sentence of which was "[Professor Banfield's book] is a piece of shit," and the rest of which was worse, so I wrote No, and said why. I find his answer very engaging—understanding, and yet resigned. "On a Vermont hillside, overlooking the Moose River, I read the review you refer to. While it didn't make me cut short my vacation, it angered and embarrassed me enough to write a curt letter to my summer replacement—I suppose I sounded stuffy myself. But I assure you this note isn't so much conciliatory as wistful. For if you were a regular reader of *The Voice*, I'm afraid you'd find many articles, alas, alas, to which you could make similar objections." . . .

Tony Bengert, who is a Maryknoll priest in Zambia, writes reacting, unhappily, to a column I had written on the meeting between Kenneth Kaunda and Edward Heath, at which Mr. Heath had informed Kaunda that yes, he, Heath, *did* intend to sell arms to South Africa, arms of the kind that can be used against white Soviet gunboats, not black freedom marchers. I had mentioned in the column that I had learned quite accidentally a year earlier, shortly before going to Zambia—primarily to oblige a friend who had a television special in mind— that I was persona non grata in Zambia, for the sin of having publicized the views of Dean Acheson on the silliness of the boycott of Rhodesia, and I expressed myself as reconciled, inasmuch as, on the whole, I would prefer to be forbidden to go to Zambia than to have to go there. Father Bengert, a terribly bright young man—I met him at Maryknoll. He was a seminarian when I spoke there a few years ago—offers an explanation of how come I was blackballed: "I'll bet some nasty USIA holdover from the last Administration, unhappy over your position in that Agency [I am a member of the United States Advisory Commission on Information]—and working in Zambia—had you declared unwanted there." . . . A gentleman from West Roxbury, Massachusetts, generally concurs with my defense of the early Beethoven, and of Bach, and wonders "whether you had explained to your youthful audience that the keyboard instrument of Bach's time made necessary so much of the decorative writing that for some ears has a fabricated sound." . . . I have a telegram from a young playwright: "Dear Mr. Buckley. The soul of a secular nation is its theater. Our theater is all but dead. I send you a modern classic tragedy and you are too busy and important to read it. How disgusting." Frances Bronson, my secretary, was very much annoyed by the telegram, because only five days earlier she had sent a letter to Peter Glenville that I had dictated. "I would not normally send along a manuscript, but I am so fetched by the vigor and grace of the letter that accompanied it (I attach it) that I wonder if you could possibly tell me whether you think it has a chance?" Frances heatedly wrote out a telegram which she proposed to send, rebuking the playwright for his impatience. I told her not to send it, because I react against declamatory rudeness that is coercive in intent—obviously the playwright thought that his telegram would get him some action. (The following week Peter told me that the author was talented but the play, in his opinion, was not ready for commercial production. I assume he is a very young man, I said, the telegram in mind. "If he isn't," Peter replied, "then you will have to counsel him to stop writing plays.")

Anyway, artists are as they are, and a lot of them simply don't follow the normal rules of conduct. When as a very young man I found myself the editor-in-chief of *National Review*, I realized two things. One, that if I had been ten years older my colleagues might well have declined to rally around a magazine of which I was to be editor and sole owner—traditional professional resentments are not felt toward people who are much younger and are fit objects for patronizing—and, two, artists are worse, but intellectuals are often bad enough, and what it comes down to is this—that concerning *certain* things, *everyone* is inaccessible to reason, and the trick is to find out what those things are, and simply accept the given in the situation.

Russell Kirk, for instance, must not under any circumstance be asked to review a movie or a television show, and to suggest to James Burnham that he read a particular book is almost to guarantee that he will not read it; that kind of thing. Sometimes—we are back on artists now—you face a concrete social problem, and yesterday, facing such a one, I wrote to a friend in Switzerland. "It occurs to me that you have sought by your silence to communicate your displeasure with me. I find that too bad, particularly since I am by all odds the nicest man I know. However, I do think that in order to save us embarrassment, we ought to know ahead of time whether, on my return to Switzerland [where I spend February and March], we are supposed, on happening upon each other, to exchange only Averted Gazes, because my Averted Gaze is a little rusty, and needs some practicing up. Or, we can resume our amiable relationship, wherein you admire my prose, I admire your art, and we agree to leave moot the question of your business acumen. Why don't we leave it this way, that if I do not hear from you in response to this letter, I shall regretfully assume that the former is your election? My love to the girls [his wife, daughter, and dog, who is Rowley's second cousin]."

There are the routine requests, all of which I regularly resolve to handle with form letters, but how to compose a form letter adequate to the resources of some writers, particularly the very young ones? "Well, here I am again. Yes sir, it takes more than a broken typewriter to keep this kid down. This is my third letter to you . . . But gee-wiz golly-darn Mr. Buckley, when are you going to answer my letters? To totally ignore a 17 year old high school conservative, I must warn you, could prove to be

17

dangerous. We are not only relatively rare but also very sensitive. After all if you keep ignoring my letters I might get the idea you don't want young people in the conservative movement. Wouldn't that be terrible? (The answer is 'yes'). But if you ignore me you are ignoring more than a young conservative. Your [sic] ignoring a young conservative from Indiana. A Cardinal Sin! . . . But Hark! All is not lost. And to prove to you I am not really sore I am going to give you this chance to make-up with me and the state of Indiana (both of whom have been ignored too long). You, Mr. Buckley, are cordially invited to be the guest speaker at our high school's Good Government Day program . . . Please understand that Key Club is a service organization for high school boys and as such we wouldn't be able to pay the high price that I know you normally get . . ."

He gets a non-form letter, the key sentence of which is, "Whenever you are disposed to be sore at me, try to remember that *National Review* is available to you for five or six dollars a year in part because of activities I undertake which result in my having to answer rather briefly notes from such pleasant people as yourself, and say no to nonpaying invitations to speak." . . . A form letter suffices for "I am writing a term paper in high school about Communism in America. I would appreciate it if you would send me some information about this subject. My teacher told me that you are a conservative who is probably a strong anti-Communist." *The teacher would not have got a form letter.* . . . The *Notre Dame* LAWYER wants a review of Ramsey Clark's book, *Crime in America:* "Upon publication of a review, we would be glad to send you fifty complimentary copies of the review, and a

18

one-year subscription to the LAWYER." I have always thought that the most genial of all form letters is the one that suggests that the correspondent did not get through, so that he won't therefore feel that his persuasiveness was met, and resisted. Whence, "Mr. Buckley has asked me to interdict all requests for interviews. articles, reviews, etc., for the next period—probably about six months, as he is drastically in arrears on commitments he has already made. I hope you will understand that to take on any further commitments at this point simply means failing to keep those he has already made. Thank you for writing. Very truly yours, Francés Bronson." . . . Then, what is about as hard-a-sell as I ever get, from the student government head of DePauw. An elaborate wind-up. "Surely this letter will rank among the very oddest of the wide and weird assortment which no doubt floats your way each week. I am writing to attempt to persuade you to accept a speaking engagement here. Please hear me out— if it's of any consequence, I've shown you the same courtesy countless times in your columns and books—in spite of profound philosophical disagreements." Then about DePauw, and how important it is. But, however good the education at DePauw, there is "one glaring defect: the absence of an even reasonable articulate conservative spokesman." The letter goes on. "It is entirely possible— nay, probable—that the overwhelming majority of De Pauw students graduating in the last decade have *never heard* so much as a syllable from an intelligent conservative." And a little guarded flattery. "Do not think me a flatterer [the word "flatterer" comes out charmingly home-typed, which I always like: something like "flatteret"]; *you* know you are intelligent—why should I

19

pretend [sic] *I* don't? To these people the term conservatism (please forgive this unavoidable use of labels) conjures up images of Hoosier anti-communist hysteria or (worse) the editorial pages of the Chicago *Tribune* and Indianapolis *Star,* intimately connected with this institution—on both of which many students here have been spoon-fed from infancy.

"The deleterious effects of this homogenized diet are several: slow-witted conservative students here are imbued with the fuzziest sorts of ideas about American society and are rendered utterly incapable of defending themselves intellectually against even a mediocre liberal spokesman. (Let us face facts: it does not require overwhelming philosophical utensils to make intellectual puree out of the grade triple-Z grist cranked out by the *Tribune* and *Star.*) Perceptive conservative students become either bored with or nauseated by such drivel and abandon the conservative cause for the better articulated, more sophisticated, and more popular liberal theses available in abundance through the media and other sources (e.g. university faculty). Liberal students all along the intelligence gradient acquire a sense of smugness and self-righteousness, and grow intellectually paunchy due to a dearth of skillful conservative sparring partners.

"We are not a wealthy organization. We can afford very little beyond your travel and associated expenses, plus perhaps a small honorarium (no doubt a pittance compared to what you could usually command). However we can promise a capacity turn-out, excellent coverage by the mass media, and unlimited flexibility—you can pick any date you wish. *Please,* give this a moment's consideration." . . . I did, of course, and decided not to

20

take on the student body president of DePauw University on the question of the triple-Z incapacity of the chief editorial writers of the Chicago *Tribune* and the Indianapolis *Star*, both of them Phi Beta Kappas from rather exacting universities; that kind of argument one simply hasn't time for. "Your letter touched me," I wrote. "I say that quite sincerely. But you must consider my situation. I work overtime so as to be able to send *National Review* to anybody who wants it for approximately $12.00 per year. [The disparity in the cited cost is because, for students, we have a crazy-rate system, which reduces the subscription price by a couple of dollars.] It costs us approximately $20 a year to produce it. The difference is made up by fund appeals and my own activities as a lecturer. The obvious answer to your generic question is: If your fellow students have any intellectual curiosity at all, they will pick up *National Review* at a very small cost to them. If they want me personally, what they want is theater. [A deucedly good point, what?] For theater, I charge—and remit my earnings to *National Review*. I don't like to say it because it sounds self-serving, but there are over five hundred applications from colleges willing to pay the full fee [I exaggerate. More like 200], and it would not be fair to penalize *National Review* by patronizing DePauw, however much I am inclined to do so as a result of your own eloquence. It is not the same thing, but I would be very happy if you would lunch with me next time you come to New York."

No answer would ever come to my answer; that often happens. The kids are, a lot of them, first-rate at turning on the charm when they want something. And then, win or lose, they deploy their charm elsewhere. I believe in

21

thank-you letters, and I have a tickler-system that reminds me when a delinquent institution writes to me for a speech, or article. The all-time offenders are the graduate students, who manage to get free speeches from you as you succumb to their sycophantic embraces, and then you never hear from them again, like the girl in any de Maupassant story. Ah, but I have learned, have I learned. The Dean of the Graduate School at Princeton, an irresistible liberal of charming habits, now calls in the student lecture head, or that is my impression, and dictates to him the thank-you letter he is to send me after my dutiful appearances there, free gratis, every couple of years, a murderous habit I fell into in the fifties, before I got around to composing my super-form letters. *I am waiting to be asked back by a certain organization at Harvard . . .*

We pull into 73rd Street, and squirm out. Jerry, the driver, will drop Peter off at his apartment, then take my column and the tape with my correspondence to Frances, and be back in time to take me to the studio. I go quickly upstairs to read as fast as I can the inexhaustible dockets of information Aggie has put together for me. I must write notes to consult during the programs, and I must write four-hundred-word introductions—one for the two Catholic college presidents, one for the Assistant U.S. Attorney General, which I read out as the program begins. I have a sandwich, a half bottle of wine, and pop a Ritalin into my mouth—a mini-stimulant prescribed for me as among the low-blood-pressured after a haunting experience in the fall of 1965 when I fainted (first and only time) at a restaurant, and was dragged off in an ambulance to Bellevue, with two or three friends who did what they could to conceal my identity (I was running for mayor of New York City), where a series of young night-doctors poked about dispiritedly, the first of them having been disappointed to learn, on examining my eyes with a laser beam, that my trouble was not an ulcer.

Off to 1481 Broadway for the taping. Jerris Leonard is bright, cunning, has ready for you the answers to the questions he expects to hear ("Why is the Nixon Administration determined to enforce integration?" "The Nixon Administration is determined to enforce the law."), and stumbles only when you say to him, Is it fair to generalize that the North is being spared the pains of massive educational integration, only because it had the foresight to insist on residential segregation years ago? Well, he said, that is to be sure how it works out, the South being where forced school integration follows from the fact of there being no residential segregation. But it does not sound very good. He is very able. . . . The priest and the nun spar, but it is only after the program is over that Father Baker accosts me to whisper, "How can Sister say that it makes no difference to the curriculum that hers is a Catholic college? What about the natural law? Metaphysics? Epistemology? How can you divorce a Catholic college from Catholicism? I mean how *can* you, even if you try?" I had asked the Sister whether, twenty or fifty years hence, they might say of Manhattanville that it was a Catholic college even as Yale was once a Congregationalist college? I had thought that this would sorely inconvenience her, in the light of her dilemma, which is at once to please the Catholic alumnae, and the anti-denominationalist Board of Regents of the State of New York.

23

She smiled sweetly, and said that who knows, that perhaps is precisely what would be said about Manhattanville; and I wondered, so ready was her response, whether she had time to invoke the help of the Holy Ghost in formulating it . . . The panelists were rather restrained. Jeff Greenfield, for whom I have a furtive fondness, is the searing radic-lib, the senior member. That was the 226th program of *Firing Line*, and I think he came on at approximately show 127. He went from Yale Law School (where he wrote an extravagant denunciation of me for the *Alumni Magazine*, and promptly got offers from N.Y. publishers to do articles, books, and encyclopaedias) to Bobby Kennedy, for whom he wrote speeches; then to John Lindsay, for whom he did the same thing (same speeches?), and now he is on his own, free-lancing and book-writing. Very quick on the draw, now and then a trace of callowness, which is quite right in someone who is his age, that bright, and that irrepressible. I reproached him only once, when he called a guest stupid; and he saw the point, and was contrite. He is very stern, ideology-wise; but he missed by a whisker the total immersion in the religion of dissent of the radicals who are two or three years younger, who believe that to smile in the company of the enemy is already to make irretrievable concessions. Jeff will smile, and I do not mean the kind of smile that you would wrest out of Molotov. He was easy on Leonard, perhaps in part for tactical reasons, Greenfield being foremost among the anti-Nixonites. It is hardly helpful to his cause to pick on young Leonard, the villain of the South which he has worked, under Nixon, so industriously to integrate.

I go directly to Al Dinegar, for the unhappiest hour of

24

my week, the Mortification of the Flesh, freshman division. Forty-five minutes of body exercises, fifteen minutes of self-defense. Al is an enormous, kindly, cunning man who teaches physical training at the Police Academy, and somehow manages to remember, without having taken notes, exactly how many push-ups you managed last week. He is big on weight-lifting, but he specifies that you must lie on your back, to do what he calls a bench-press, to avoid strain. "All right, Bill, let's have ten of these if you can, otherwise eight." He agrees to wait until The Beatles strike a galvanizing upbeat on the tape recorder I have installed in a corner of the tiny gym to help take my mind off the pain and tedium of it all. Unfortunately, Al has no sense of rhythm whatsoever—he admits this and I take it that his wife, on the dance floor, is eloquent on the subject—so he has to watch me very carefully to accent the cue, inasmuch as I consider it a part of our contract that I need not begin hoisting the one hundred and five pound weight until I and the music are synchronized. I make it to eight, not to ten, and I am truly distressed because I have never failed to make my quota before. Al tells me that there are variations in an individual's physical condition from day to day which would easily account for the discrepancy, but he is unable to tell me why I should not have come upon this variation before, and he says perhaps I have a low-grade germ or something that is eating up a little of my strength. In due course he shows me a technique for dislodging a man who is lying across my torso. It is very simple, requiring only that you remember *not* to use your neck muscles, else strain can result. My son, Christopher, took an hour a day from Al a fortnight ago, before leaving as a deck hand on a steamer going around the world, and during the fourth session, he inadvertently disregarded Al's advice, but, as is Christopher's way—as is the way of every 18-year-old—he reassured Al that the consequences of disobeying him were clearly exaggerated; the trouble being that the next day he was not able to raise his head. The boxing comes at a moment of maximum exhaustion, one's muscles having had a total workout, so that merely to keep up one's arms is painful, though we manage a little sparring, and I am obliged to admit it, that for the few seconds that my stamina would last, Al has made me a most dangerous instrument, should anyone try to push me onto a subway track, or gouge out my eyes, or toss me off the Empire State Building (NOBODY should EVER try to force me over the top of the Empire State Building. I would be the LAST person HE ever tried to force over the top of the Empire State Building), it being however important to remember not to use the techniques that Al teaches you, merely, say, to punctuate a point during a political discussion.

Then to 73rd. We are going to hear the last of the three concerts organized by Rosalyn Tureck, the first two having featured her on the harpsichord and the piano, tonight's featuring twenty-three string instrumentalists whom she will conduct in *The Art of Fugue*. I love Rosalyn. I never thought I would ever be referring to her as "Rosalyn," having worshipped her from afar for many years. But I thought two months ago to do a television program called "Why Are They Afraid of Bach?" *They* meaning the kids, the principal point I wanted to furrow being that much of the music they *do* listen to is as exacting as much of Bach's music. I can understand people who cannot listen to Bach because they cannot go beyond Kostelanetz; but some of the stuff that nowadays engrosses many of the young people I myself find extremely difficult to understand, and that is the point I wanted to talk about. When first the idea of having her on the program came up, we didn't commit ourselves to having her on alone, not knowing whether she was articulate; so I asked her for lunch one day, and she quite bowled me over. She is utterly articulate, and also warm and radiant, and has a superb sense of fun. I raised the point as we sat, before lunch, that there are those who believe that Bach is lacking in emotion, and she rose haughtily and sat down on the piano bench striking off a passage from an *English Suite*—slow chords, a heart-tearingly poignant theme—and then turned, demanding to know how could *anybody* without the *deepest* springs of emotion compose what she had just played? We agreed on the format, and that she would play a total of four times—for a cumulative period of seven and a half minutes, as it turned out; and when, without rehearsal, two weeks later, the program was over, and I handed her the wilted bundle of flowers Warren had hidden behind my chair, the great Tureck, whose artistic restraint has been so much commended, responded by throwing her arms about me and giving me a kiss. "I really think you would leave me in a minute for that woman," my wife remarked later, and I grinned sheepishly, which is the way to handle Pat when she is being outrageous.

Warren Steibel was there at 73rd, and his friend the composer Leonard Kastle; Sophie Wilkins, an editor of Alfred Knopf, whom I came to know (and love) when she wrote a few years ago asking if she could help Edgar Smith, my friend who is in the Death House at Trenton; Frances Bronson, Aggie Schmidt, and C. Dickerman Williams and his wife, Virginia. Dick is my lawyer on most matters. He is seventy and, technically, retired, though no one knows the difference between the habits of pre- and post-retired Williams. He and I could have got a great deal more accomplished over the years, except that we always laugh together, about one half the time. I have referred to him publicly as "the greatest lawyer in the world," as matter-of-factly as if he had won that title unequivocally, like Joe Louis, and although he is an aristocrat of impeccable manner, sometime editor of the Yale Law School journal, clerk to Chief Justice William Howard Taft, general counsel to the Department of Commerce, a lawyer's lawyer, who has in him that little touch of elfin abandon which if Herbert Hoover had it, he'd have been President of the United States on the day he died. We have champagne and sandwiches, planning to eat supper after the concert, at the Russian Tea Room. Dick raises his glass and proposes a toast to his wife, whose birthday it turns out to be. I had invited them to join us for the concert only at noon, just before the TV, and if I had known I'd have baked a cake, I said, and we went off happily into the car, after the usual struggle with Rowley, who thought he would be getting his sixth car trip of the day. The performance of *The Art of Fugue* was, simply, perfect. I enjoyed it less than I hoped I would, because I arrived grumpy at the prospect of an evening with Rosalyn Tureck during which she would not strike a note on the piano; and because I thought the ensemble over-full, a point I made the mistake of telling Rosalyn a

28

few nights later. The Williamses would not join us at the Tea Room, since his regimen is tightly controlled and calls for him to be in bed by eleven. We parted on the street, and I said to Virginia that next time, she should give me a little warning when her birthday is coming up, as it had been all I was able to do, this time on such short notice, to hire Carnegie Hall, and prevail on Rosalyn Tureck to assemble a concert. She hesitated for just a second's confusion, then laughed, and went off with the greatest lawyer in the world, while we went in to have blinis and vodka. And then a cab, a little reading, and to sleep.

TUESDAY. A couple of hours with the correspondence Frances sent up late yesterday. I have a reply from General McPherson of The National War College. He had written asking me to participate in "one of the most popular and stimulating features of the annual course of instruction at The National War College," to wit their "evening lecture program" which "is attended not only by our faculty and students and their wives, but also by other guests from the Washington area. Therefore, we give particular attention to selection of the speaker for each of these occasions. . . . It has been more than a decade since you addressed a National War College audience. We do hope that we shall have the opportunity of welcoming you back." I had been waiting for such a letter, I have to confess it, for several years. I replied: "Dear General McPherson: I must suppose that you did not find it easy to write me the letter you did, observing that it has been a decade since I addressed The National War

College. It prompts me to ask, Where has The War College been during the decade? I recognize that you were not (presumably) personally responsible for choking off invitations to conservative anti-Communist speakers during the early sixties, but although I am a child in military strategy, I recognize an operation when I see one. I have heard it variously ascribed to Drew Pearson, William Fulbright, and Arthur Schlesinger—the ban by The National War College on invitations to a certain class of dissenting lecturers. Although we all recognize the supremacy of the civil arm, it would be reassuring to learn that, at The National War College, they also teach the virtue of valor, and I continue to hope that future historians will discover that the Commandant of The National War College did not surrender without a fight . . . Under the circumstances, I am not inclined, after the long banishment, to perform at an affair primarily social, for a fee which is a very small fraction of the fee I command. If you desire me to speak as I did before, at a working session of The War College, I shall accept that invitation as in the line of duty."

To that letter he has replied, "As Commandant I have full autonomy in speaker selection, and with the advice of the senior faculty, endeavor to maintain the vital 'balanced' expression of views. Actually I only came to the College last July, but have found no evidence of the 'ban' you mentioned." He then lists some "conservative anti-Communist" speakers who appeared during the sixties, among them Senator Goldwater and Hans Morgenthau, and renews the invitation, only this time to address a working session. I now reply that I "do not seek a confrontation, nor would I go so far as to suggest that every

30

anti-Communist in America disappeared from your speaking program—that would be preposterous. It is a fact that five of the six people mentioned by Drew Pearson in that particular column [I was mistaken about the author—it was a Madison *Capital Times* writer, not Drew Pearson], who had lectured regularly, year after year, were not invited again." I agree to go, and I congratulate myself on the delicacy with which I desist from giving the names of the people I have in mind—what is the point of embarrassing the general?

. . . Lawrence Fertig had reminded me a while back that Earle Holsapple is resigning as Treasurer of the Historical Research Foundation—a tiny organization that operates on one hundred and fifty thousand dollars in capital allotted to it by the late Alfred Kohlberg, who was much publicized during the fifties by *The Reporter* magazine, and others, as "The China Lobby"—and asked that I compose a tribute to the man who resisted all efforts to make him invest The Foundation's funds in the market. "WHEREAS," I wrote, "the said Mr. Holsapple, resisting all temptations to imprudence, did manage the funds of the Historical Research Foundation with maximum effect in a conservative but wonderfully durable portfolio; and WHEREAS by so doing, he did make an ass out of our beloved former colleague Alex Hillman, who presumed to instruct our Treasurer in the uses of the stock market; and WHEREAS our Treasurer Mr. Holsapple has on the occasion of his 84th birthday elected to relinquish his duties" then therefore, etc., etc. Now Larry Fertig says he has taken the liberty of slightly modifying a particular phrase, "following the old conservative maxim *de mortuis nil nisi bonum*." (Alex Hillman is dead.) Sure. I remember how it enraged Alfred Kohlberg when Dean Acheson quoted the maxim as a reason for not commenting on the death of Joe McCarthy. I always thought it a devilish rhetorical device. In order to mean anything at all, the maxim should say, *De mortuis nil nisi bonum, ergo.* . . . Otherwise, you have paralepsis, pure and simple. I assume Dean Acheson understood that, but I am not absolutely sure. What would he have said *good* about Joe McCarthy at that point? Other than that he had been obliging enough to die? . . . And a letter from Edgar Eisenhower, concerning another foundation, my all-time favorite. A gentleman called Gaty, who lived and worked in Wichita, Kansas, as an independent oil operator and executive for Beech Aircraft Corporation, died a few years ago, a bachelor, and a philanthropist. He gave the bulk of his estate to nephews cousins retainers, and to several charities. Then he spun off about a million and a half dollars into a self-liquidating ten-year trust, to be devoted to helping tax-exempt organizations preferably of the kind that engaged in conservative educational activity, and then he named the trustees. J. Edgar Hoover; Senators Frank Lausche, Strom Thurmond, John Tower, Barry Goldwater; Clarence Manion, former Dean of the Notre Dame Law School; George Benson, President of Harding College; Edgar Eisenhower and myself. On reaching this point in the letter from the executor I remember wondering why Mr. Gaty had not also named the Pope, and Lord Salisbury, for all the chance there was of convening such a group anywhere, let alone in Wichita, on any single day. But wait. The old gentleman had not flourished in Wichita by witlessness. There would be one annual meeting, the executor explained, in Wichita; each trustee

32

would receive a one thousand dollar fee for attending it, and would have the absolute right, unquestioned, to allocate ten thousand dollars to any tax deductible organization of his choice. The balance of the money that matured over the years would be distributed according to majority vote. Result? On a Saturday, in the late fall, in Wichita, Kansas, at eight-thirty in the morning, nine men cross the street from their hotel to the Fourth National Bank Building, and anyone who happens to look up at them would guess that here indeed was the seventh day of May. Mr. Hoover never came, and an alternate was selected, who votes his ten thou to the J. Edgar Hoover Foundation. But all the rest come, indeed have never missed. Sometimes they will come in five minutes before the meeting begins, dropping out of the sky in a Lear jet. John Tower usually arrives ten minutes late, and I secretly suspect that his motive is to miss the invocation with which Chairman Thurmond opens the meeting. It wasn't until this year that there was an absentee—Edgar Eisenhower, the world's single most charming man. He had a cold, and his absence, under the rigorous rules of the Trust, left him without a vote. I moved that in consideration of his illness, we vote to allocate ten thousand dollars to the same causes to which Mr. Eisenhower had allocated his ten thousand at the previous meeting, and the proposal was carried unanimously. Cast thy bread upon the waters. Mr. Eisenhower writes to say thanks, and to add, "I wish the bank would hold its meeting earlier in the year because November is becoming a little cold for my tender flesh." Actually, that won't do, because "a little earlier in the year" means election season, and that would not suit the convenience of the senators. . . .

33

The clips continue to pour in on Jimmy's election. *Newsweek* prepared a cover story on Jim, electing at the last moment to devote it to Senator Muskie. But the research was done, and I see now that the San Antonio *Light* has run a piece by Tom Mathews and Jacquin Sanders, sent out by "Newsweek Feature Service" (of which I hadn't heard), on the family. The day after the election, Tom Mathews rode with me from *National Review* to Syosset, Long Island, where I had to give a speech, and now I see a part of what I told him coming in through the clip. The theme of the cover story, Mathews had told me in some embarrassment, was to be the similarity between the Kennedys and the Buckleys, a so-what point that people have been making for a long time, giving way to the reticulative passions that seem to me to rule not only journalism, but sociology and even psychology. The story quotes me directly: " 'We do have similarities to the Kennedys,' says Bill. 'Our wealth, our fecundity, our Catholicism. Other than that, the comparison is engaging but misleading. The Kennedys had an Irish cultural upbringing. I didn't know where Ireland was until I graduated from Yale.' The truth is," the story goes on, "the Buckleys are not the Irish-Catholics they are thought to be. On the maternal side, the heritage is Southern with Robert E. Lee in the background. And their paternal great-grandfather, who emigrated from Ireland, was an Irish Protestant who converted when he married."

Why are so many Irish defensive? How can anybody be patronizing about Ireland, in the century when Ireland gave us Shaw and Joyce and Yeats, while England was defending herself primarily through American expatriates James and Eliot? But to go around posing as an

"Irish-American" ought to suggest something. What? In our youth we were much more heavily influenced by Mexico, where Father lived for twenty years before being expelled, than by Ireland, which he visited for the first time in 1939 because he wanted to see the horse show at Dublin. The five youngest of us spoke Spanish before we learned English (and in between, three of us spoke French). The eldest five went from French to Spanish to English. A dull point, I always thought, the Kennedy-Buckley business, but there will probably be no end of it. . . . A priest writes to tell me that he would be glad to give me a list of people to see in Chile. I had mentioned in my column that I would be traveling there, making the point that not to do so in the next period is rather like giving up a retrospective opportunity to visit Havana in January of 1959. He concludes, "If you make this trip to Chile, I would like you to meet the Chile I know, and not the Chile that you could be introduced to by the American Embassy. There is a world of difference!" The last sentence suggests that the priest meant to write: ". . . and not the Chile that you *would* be introduced to by the American Embassy." Why the difference, I wonder. Oh, I mean why the difference other than the obvious difference, that ambassadors and priests don't meet the identical set of people? Is it the suggestion that ambassadors as a genre don't know what is really happening in Chile? Or that this particular ambassador doesn't know? I doubt the latter, because Ed Korry is bright and industrious, a very good friend and former colleague of my sister Priscilla, the managing editor of *National Review*. She used to work for United Press, under Ed in both New York and Paris. Ed is a most resolute liberal, who used to tease and be teased by members of the family while weekending in Sharon, which he often did. I spoke to him over the telephone last week while he was in Washington to discuss the crisis. I am to stay with him at the residence, he insisted, but probably I should have an official address at a downtown hotel—he will arrange it all. . . . I must decide, at some point, whether to charge my airline ticket to the USIA, or pay for it myself. The members of the Commission are instructed by Congress and the President to travel, to survey our operations all over the world, and to report back our findings. Jack Anderson, Drew Pearson's successor, reported in his column a few months ago that the USIA had paid about $3,500 in airplane bills for me in the year or so since I was appointed by Nixon, even though I wrote professionally from everywhere I went. How evil that sounds, or is made to sound! I keep reminding myself that as long as I think I am doing the right thing, I mustn't let Drew Pearson-types intimidate me. If I had been Tom Dodd, I'd have organized, in response to Drew Pearson, the biggest possible testimonial dinner in my own behalf, $100 a plate, the proceeds going directly to me, as an unrestricted gift, the whole of it printed plainly on the ticket. Drew Pearson-types flourish from the special difficulty of communicating certain kinds of truths, for instance that the incremental trip across the Atlantic Ocean, say to attend a meeting of Public Affairs Officers in Vienna, isn't *fun*. It is *work*. If you spend half your life on airplanes anyway, the extra plane ride somebody else pays for isn't a *treat*. But you can't *say that*, because you will sound either blasé, and spoiled; or disingenuous. And sitting all day, listening to eight hours of reports on the Voice of

America, cultural exchange programs, magazine distribution problems, library attendance records isn't *fun*. It may be and often is *interesting*, like seminars on the Common Market. But it isn't *fun*; it is *duty*, and in the case of the Commission, unpaid duty. But already Anderson has won a victory, because here I am dwelling on the point . . .

Gene Tunney has called me twice, and I had better drop him a note, since, on trying to return his call, I find he is out of the office. The last time he called he was wondering what exactly was the meaning of the legend on Yeats's tombstone, "Cast a cold eye/On life, on death./Horseman, pass by!" I didn't have the least idea, but that very evening I was on my boat with Hugh Kenner and I asked him. He said, with that precision I find utterly endearing, that by coincidence I had asked the question of one of the half-dozen people in the world (T. S. Eliot called Hugh the finest critic of his generation) who happen to know. I'd have been a little apprehensive if Gene's call had come in a month ago, because (of course) *National Review* supported George Murphy against his son John; and Gene has been a very old friend and supporter of *NR* . . . I write a letter commending a young man who used to sail with us—for a position in a major hospital; a young man of striking intelligence and affability, who went on to graduate first in his class at medical school. How *do* admissions types, whether of universities or hospitals or yacht clubs, manage to evaluate these letters? Do they develop a kind of Braille, by which they can tell if you are being effusive because you mean to be effusive; or that you are being effusive because diplomacy requires that you be effusive? My device is to say what I have to say, and then invite the addressee

37

to telephone me to probe for further details, intending thereby to register the seriousness of my endorsement. I remember in 1966 receiving a request for a seconding letter from the sponsor of Franklin Delano Roosevelt Jr. for membership in the New York Yacht Club, my only personal experience with Mr. Roosevelt having been that he was on *Firing Line* a few weeks earlier, shortly after running for governor of New York, and getting fewer votes than the Conservative candidate, Paul Adams—the historic moment that gave the Conservatives the Third Position on the ballot. I was surprised on that count— that I knew him only so briefly; and on the larger count, my assumption having been that the New York Yacht Club was surely invented, a hundred or two hundred years ago, by an antecedent of FDR Jr., and I would have thought that my own inclinations on the matter of his proposed membership would have been a) supererogatory; or b) ideologically suspect. I settled the dilemma by advising the Membership Committee that my own feeling was that Mr. Roosevelt ought to be admitted ex officio to any organization that his father had neglected to nationalize. No letter of thanks, or acknowledgment, though I had concluded by saying the truth, which is that even after introducing Mr. Roosevelt on the television program as a man who has "specialized in being a has-been," I had nonetheless found him greatly charming and courteous, which may have been hard for him under the circumstances . . . A friend writes me, "Mario Procaccino has had to take a little flack from Democratic colleagues who contrast the publicized thanks he received at Rockefeller HQs with the unpublicized thanks he received from the conservatives." I pass along the note to

38

Dan Mahoney, the chairman of the Conservative Party, *National Review*'s lawyer, and my friend . . . A young girl, a close follower of *Firing Line* (she is a secretary, but she has not missed one of the last one hundred screenings done in New York—how she arrived at such an arrangement with her employer I do not know, and shall not ask), tells me that she has reason to believe that a prominent CBS television commentator, whom I came to know slightly during the mayoralty campaign, is lonely following a personal tragedy, so I write to him and suggest we lunch . . . Dick Clurman of *Time* sends in the headline on the suicide of Mishima and suggests that here is a Conservative who knows how to make his points with style. That reminds me, and I send off a note to Gerhart Niemeyer, whose Letter from Tokyo in the current issue of *National Review*, which at the last moment we had to go over to put references to Mishima in the past tense, is superb; everything about Gerhart is superb, a judgment in which his students appear to agree. I have to leave for the office.

I stop by at Dr. Poster's on the way to the editorial conference, for a routine fitting of my contact lenses, with which I have been playing for 18 months because that long ago, coincident with my failing eyesight, my friend Renira Horne told me about the pleasures of contact lenses—you put them on in the morning, take them off at night, and in between it is as though your eyes had never deteriorated. Then Ronald Reagan encouraged me, telling me that he has to remind himself to take his off at night. Dr. Poster is the Number 5 doctor I have consulted on the matter, my experiences in between having served primarily to amuse my wife, who urges me to give them up, as snares and delusions, even as she knows that such taunts harden the determination, although I guess I should acknowledge the distinction between "the determination" and "my determination," there being a distinction. Dr. Poster is the chairman of the contact lens section of his profession, and he is the most sublimely confident practitioner in the world, who, when I asked him, informed me that he disqualifies about 10 per cent of those who approach him for lenses, upon discovering among other things a hypersensitivity or whatever to foreign bodies introduced onto the eye, and that of those he proceeds to deal with, he fails in only about 10 per cent of the cases. He is a very patient man, who expects me to show up week after week (this is my fifth or sixth visit) on the joint understanding that the experiment is a failure unless I can dispense altogether with the eyeglasses I began to need only a few years ago. I tell him, today, that I am greatly discouraged by the *Reader's Digest* article Aggie showed me, written by experts in the business who say that seven hours is the most you can hope to wear the lenses at one time. Dr. Poster smiles, puffs at his cigarette (he is trying to cut down because he has been the principal chain smoker in America for many years), and tells me that that is nonsense. Removing the lenses reminds me of the humiliations of my apprenticeship. It was Vienna, and I was locked in with the USIA, when my lenses began to itch uncontrollably. I endeavored to remove them unobserved, while Ambassador Douglas MacArthur II was briefing the twenty of us. Soon I became aware that I was being noticed, and that it wouldn't be long before the USIA officials concluded that I suffered from an uncon-

40

trollable facial disorder. I walked quietly out, came upon a large Marine security guard, begged his pardon, handed him a rubber plunger, and asked him to please extract the lens from my eye; which he proceeded deftly to do, having laid aside his machine gun. There were other such experiences, but I have become a fanatic, and am always telling my skeptical friends that in Japan children are automatically fitted with contact lenses, in preference to eyeglasses—or so I am told—the advantages being obvious. As an evangelist, I suffer only from my failure to have been fitted with a set that I can, at this point, happily put on early in the morning, and remove late at night. I shall one day, under the burden of the taunts of my skeptical wife, especially cherish the sweetness of the chime, when I turn off the bedside light, "Ducky, did you remember to take out your lenses?" Dr. Poster, who does his own adjustments on the spot, makes a tiny adaptation, and sends me off happily confident that this will prove to be the marginal adaption; which it isn't.

James Burnham comes in from Kent, Connecticut, on the eleven o'clock Tuesday train, which is why we do not hold our editorial meeting until eleven-thirty, or soon thereafter. There are eight or nine of us, seated around the table. Burnham is senior, a founding editor of the magazine, revered from the beginning by all of us, not only because of the legend—at 25 he was a full professor of philosophy at NYU; he stopped people dead with his *Managerial Revolution* early in the forties—but because of his quiet professionalism. He wrote the first piece on jazz for *Partisan Review*, and would write tomorrow on the common roots between phrenology and astrology, and the editorial transaction would be as simple as my saying, Jim, would you handle that, say, a No. 3? A No. 3 means a short editorial, a No. 1 being the longest.

Bill Rusher always speaks first, because as publisher he goes back to other business after making his recommendations. He is the showman—who, as he ticks off his list, writes the appropriate commentary on each item with the tone of his voice, and takes special pleasure from reading aloud choice news items or speeches or releases from his most particular enemies, liberal Republicans. His timing is so good that his final sentence usually ends as he reaches the door of the conference room, which he opens with a flourish, his departure the signal for monotony to begin.

Jeffrey Hart comes down from Dartmouth, where he teaches eighteenth century English, history and poetry; writes a syndicated column; and produces a couple of books per year.

Priscilla, who as managing editor (I summoned her years ago from her post at UPI in Paris to help her younger brother) coordinates everything, reads—as will everyone around the table—from a list of items she thinks need editorial treatment, and you can see the writers run lines through the items that she has anticipated.

We go around the table. The tradition that points of view should not be explicated at the conference is apparently overwhelming, so much so that recently a very young assistant editor approached my sister Pitts after a meeting, telling her that he had been assigned, simply, "Burma." "What *is* our point of view on Burma?" he asked. I am fascinated by how the editorial conference determines the lay of the editorial emphasis. What-is-our-position-on-Burma very seldom happens, because the position on Burma seems somehow to spring naturally out of the loins of the magazine. A position arrived at in this way must be distinguished from the decision-making process of, say, the editors of the *Daily World,* whose line is easily developed by merely plopping the question into lay-away chemicals. *NR's* is a quite unusual process, particularly in the light of the disparate emphases of its principal spirits. Frank Meyer, although he is never present—he lives reclusively in Woodstock, New York, as columnist and book review editor—is the relentless libertarian and global anti-Communist. Jeffrey is the flypaper who picks up the lint of any cultural development, anywhere, and it is never so amorphous, when he sits down to write about it, that it cannot fuel his heavy-duty engines. Priscilla has her eye out for the piquancies, and for the sentimental attachments of *National Review.* ("The trouble with conservatives," Robert Strausz-Hupé once said, "is they do not retrieve their wounded".) Chris Simonds, our Woodstock Nation, alternates between Understanding, and Anathematizing, and John Coyne is our California kid-watcher. He is very pleased this morning because a half hour ago he got a phone call from Spiro Agnew who told him that he, Agnew, had read *The Kumquat Statement*—Coyne's account of what happened at Berkeley, and what has happened generally at the hands of the kids—and thinks it splendid, which greatly pleases John, whose first book it is, and who is smarting from reviews which contrast it unfavorably with Jim Kunen's *Strawberry Statement,* whose counterpart *Kumquat* admittedly is. John's account of the phone call is rendered as Buster Keaton would have done it, dry-face, slightly cynical, but clearly pleased; and we tingle with the thought that there is probably not another editorial office in New York City that would appreciate a congratulatory telephone call from Spiro Agnew.

We come all the way around, I make the assignments, and we disperse. A few hours later, the writers begin to channel in the copy to Priscilla who puts it into the dumbwaiter that rises one floor to my desk, where, usually not sooner than Wednesday morning, I begin to scoop it out, edit it, and then shoot it back down to Pitts for the typists. When there are very specific questions, the writer and I communicate over the telephone. Occasionally Aggie solves research problems. But the crush is under control; we have about five hours to process seven thousand words of copy, so I can afford to throw away what would take too long to correct.

I lunch in the same room with Aggie, and with Tex Lezar, and Dan Oliver. Tex graduated with honors from Yale, and needs work pending a decision on his application for a Rhodes scholarship. Dan split off from Louis Auchincloss's law firm in order to serve as a volunteer for Jim's campaign. A few years earlier Dan had arrived at my own (mayoral) campaign headquarters, fresh from law school, volunteering his time at the lick-envelope level. He went to school with Jim Burnham's son at Milton, then Harvard, then Fordham Law School, but the ideological juices ran, and he prevailed on Louis Auchincloss to give him the summer off to work for James Buckley. "For how long is Dan's leave of absence?" a mutual friend asked Managing Partner Auchincloss in August.

44

"Until Jim loses," the novelist replied. Now Dan, Jim having not lost, decides to ponder, for a few months, an extra-legal career, and the four of us discuss a big book I have promised, along with Aggie, to do for Viking Press; to wit, a Debater's Handbook, the guts of which will be highly researched briefs on either side of fifty controversial public issues. Our problem right this minute is that the paradigmatic chaper, on which we have been working for months, is so long that we figure the book would come to three-quarters of a million words. I need to know *right now* whether that length is simply out-size, and put in a call to Viking President Tom Guinzburg, who was a roommate at Yale during sophomore year, and who brought out my book *The Unmaking of a Mayor*. He is out of town. Reach him, I plead. He is located at a restaurant in Washington, and he comes to the telephone, asking whether I am tracking him down in order to offer him an ambassadorship. We exchange the back-and-forth, and I ask him whether Viking can hope to merchandise something of the size we are thinking about. He replies that he will need technical consultation to answer that question, and finally confesses to me that he is sitting in the anteroom of a small Hungarian restaurant, that the phone call has already paralyzed conversation throughout the restaurant, and would I *please* wait until tomorrow, when he returns to his office? That means that we cannot make other than contingent plans for the Handbook; so, another delay, so what? Publishers do not seem to care, particularly.

I go back to my desk for the phone messages. Putnam's wants me to get Jim to record his daily impressions on how-to-be-a-senator. I call him. He is interested, but

45

doubts that he can bring himself to dictate into a machine every night. It is left that he will try but will feel no obligation to Putnam's if it doesn't work out. Jim tells me, as we chat, that he has just finished conferring with Senator Javits, his upcoming senior colleague who last week announced that he would protest Jim's proposed inclusion in the Senate's Republican caucus. After all, Javits was quoted as saying, he had devoted "a lifetime" to making the Republican Party more "progressive," what now was he expected to do, the voters having sent a reactionary to the Senate, "fold"? I had written in my column, "There is one obvious solution. Since Senator Javits has devoted a lifetime to making the Republican Party of New York State what it now is not, what else can be expected of him? Two lifetimes? But it is the lot of man to have only one lifetime each, and not even a super-progressive political party can bequeath us two lifetimes. So that by the logic of Senator Javits' statement, it is altogether appropriate, indeed it is mandatory, that he should—resign." I then underscored the irony. "It occurs to me that by so doing, [Senator Javits] could revive that great dream of which he spoke so very eloquently all during the summer and fall—namely the re-election of Senator Charles Goodell. This way, Governor Rockefeller could, gamely, reappoint Senator Goodell to continue Senator Javits' lifetime attempt to liberalize the Republican Party. That way, if you follow me, Senator Javits succeeds in passing along the torch to someone whose views he approves of so roundly." Jim, having just met with Javits, tells me, "You know what he said? He said, 'You know, your brother thinks I should resign.'" I

46

didn't ask Jim, after the laughter was done, how he explained it all to the senior senator from New York. Poor Jim.

After lunch I meet with a Social Democrat, a bachelor in his late fifties, of impeccable breeding and purpose, who trains his eyes, always, on the German thing. He wants me to know how dangerous he believes Brandt's *Ostpolitik* has become, and who are the principal figures in New York who are expressing their fears privately to the State Department, and to the White House . . . Then a meeting with a former Hungarian (who no longer speaks Hungarian); a French scholar, who is the most prolific bookwriter since Georges Simenon. He is a formidable academic, who is disaffected with the Conservative Book Club and Arlington House. He has heard the rumor that I "own" the companies, and wonders, do I intend to effect any reforms, best defined as instructing them to publish more of his books? I explain that I am merely a minority stockholder and chairman of the board of a broadcasting company that bought the common stock of the two publishing companies last spring, but that even supposing I were bent on doing so, I would find it as unlikely that I could affect Arlington's policies concerning my friend's books as that I could affect them concerning books that I had already taken the initiative to promote. I came back from Russia in May overcome with enthusiasm for a book, *Message from Moscow,* that had been published a year earlier by Alfred Knopf, but got practically no notice at all. It happens to be the best book on contemporary Russia published, maybe, ever;

47

and I called the president of the Conservative Book Club, urging him to consider it for selection by the CBC. He assigned it to readers, who reported back against it, on the grounds that the (anonymous, for reasons of security) author's own prejudices, here and there revealed in the book, were in favor of socialism; and such heterodoxy a small minority of CBC readers would not tolerate, even as presumably they would not have tolerated twenty-five years ago the distribution of *Animal Farm*, in the light of Orwell's persistent inclinations to socialism. I know, I know, said my friend the president, but it is a *business* matter; because if the *smallest* minority defects, that makes the publication of the book unprofitable; and we simply *cannot survive* if we publish selections that would result in significant resignations from the Club. I understood; and my Hungarian friend confesses, ruefully, that he too understands. His other purpose has to do with his newest book, just published in French. He hopes to bring out an edition in English, but the hot American publishing prospect, before saying Yes, wants to know whether I would write the introduction. Yes, I say. Sight unseen? he asks. Sight unseen, I say—tacitly relying on the assumption that my old friend has not gone cuckoo since his other books; if he has, I can withdraw my commitment, on honorable grounds. But surely I want to read the edition that now exists in French? No, I tell him, because it is a strain for me to read French.

At that moment the telephone rings. It is the son of a Latin American dignitary whose father I used to know well. The son tells me that his father has not heard from me since writing a month ago enclosing a letter which he charged me to deliver personally into the hands of President Nixon. I explain that the letter reached me almost three weeks late because I was traveling; that the situation is very difficult; that I simply do not see the President all that frequently; that I forwarded the letter, only yesterday, to someone who would pass it along; and that I have already written to his father that I had done so, but, I ask, is the address of the Safe House set down by his father in inexact hand, quite right? and I give him my reading of it. It turns out that I have transcribed it correctly, and the son, warning me that so serious is the situation in his country that his own brother is at that moment in jail, promises to call his father, and tell him that the mission is accomplished.

The conversation had been in Spanish, a language my Hungarian friend understands (he understands every language), and with his cosmopolitan intelligence, he deduced who it was who had called, in behalf of what cause, and if he had stayed another five minutes, he'd have volunteered to write a book on *that* problem. If you can speak Spanish that easily, he persists, surely you can run through my book in French? Polyglots are that way, I find. They reach a point where every language silts up into a more or less recognizable vernacular. They find it hard to believe that someone who knows *one* foreign language will find reading a book in *any* major language a strain, let alone impossible. He agrees to let me have the manuscript when it is in English.

My accountant is next. A buoyant, expressive, energetic man, who would have been among those who counseled Ferdinand to have a fling with Columbus, the type I like; but today he is very dour, and I find myself wondering, as he tells me how extravagant I am, whether he

49

actually rehearsed, in order to make himself more convincing. He urges me not to proceed with a coveted project I have in mind, a wonderfully impractical project, and I more or less agree, admiring the grace of his Calvinism, even while knowing that if I so much as wink at him, he will fatalistically wipe away the Maginot Line as easily as he would draw down a blind, thus chaperoning me across the immobilized positions of actuarial prudence.

It is time to dine with the senior editors—a sacred and functional weekly meeting. Usually we meet at 73rd, directly from the office, but tonight we go to Paone's, around the corner, a) because Paone's is the best restaurant in New York, b) because we are bound, after Paone's, for Fillmore East, downtown. None of us has been there before. I got tickets on learning that Virgil Fox the organist would play Bach there tonight, accompanied by a "light" expert. Lights are big this season. One gathers that they greatly augment the likelihood that the audience will groove along with the soloist. I had heard Fox a year before at Philharmonic Hall, marveled at his virtuosity, and appreciated his familiarity with Bach. And I had heard about the glamor of Fillmore East, as Jim Burnham had, so we looked forward, the lot of us, to the experience. A wonderful meal, and on the way out of Paone's I am greeted by a man my own age who writes me twice a week, a reformed alcoholic, an undeniable Catholic, who a few months ago, at the urging of several of us, enrolled in a Catholic seminary particularly designed to meet the needs of former alcoholics. But, he wrote me last week, he is pulling out, no hard

50

feelings against the Church, it is merely that he has no vocation; and there he is, as we walk out, having dinner with a lady friend, a Coca-Cola by his plate of fettucine. I shake hands, and only after we are in the taxi, reflect that I have two extra tickets, Jeffrey Hart having declined to join us. But it is too late.

We arrive, and there are hippies and non-hippies trying to get in, a sell-out. One young man ventures forward, do I have an extra ticket? I give him one of the two tickets, thinking to keep the second, under the circumstances, as cordon sanitaire. We are astonished by the crowd, only a minority of which is Woodstock Nation. We learn that that is because the prices have been raised by 25 per cent. V. Fox comes on, and speaks a minute or two before each number, attempting to attract the audience to God by stressing the common wavelengths on which He, and Bach, operate. The performance is god-awful, because Fox clearly wants to impress the kids by a) the noise, and b) his virtuosity. At one point during a prelude, I am tempted to rise solemnly, commandeer a shotgun, and advise Fox, preferably in imperious German, if only I could learn German in time to consummate the fantasy, that if he does not release the goddam vox humana, which is ooing-ahing-eeing the music where Bach clearly intended something closer to a bel canto, I shall simply have to blow his head off. During the intermission, a boy and girl who serve as ushers explain the economic situation, and advise that a week hence, the owner of Fillmore East will repeat Virgil Fox at the old prices, in case I want to come back. After the intermission, Fox introduces the *Passacaglia* at Wagnerian length, almost but not quite to the point of causing mutiny in

51

the audience, whose stirrings become discernible after the fourth or fifth minute. The maestro then turns and snows them with his dexterity, which is undeniable, the problem being that it will be ten years before I can appreciate again the music he has played, so over-loud, so throbby, so plucky-wucky the portamentos, so Phil Spitalny the cantandos.

We drive home. I speculate. How come it didn't hurt Fox more than it hurt us? And Jim Burnham as usual offers the only acceptable explanation, namely, that Fox is so much the evangelist, he must have figured that it was more important to fill the house with listeners who would hear Bach for the first time than worry about those who would resolve, like me, to have heard Fox for the last time. We have a glass of champagne at Jim's, before I go home to write the column due tomorrow morning.

WEDNESDAY. Dan Mahoney comes for breakfast, to discuss pressing political questions and, we both hope, less pressing problems concerning my will. I first met him in 1954 when he was a student at Columbia Law School, before whose forum he had asked me to speak, and I agreed, but the meeting was canceled because that was the day my father had a stroke in South Carolina. Somehow we stayed in touch over the years, and I came to know his closest friend Kieran O'Doherty, who is the sword-militant of the Conservative Party, and Dan's wife, who is Kieran's sister.

Dan is most easily described, among the politicians of this world, as a bird of paradise. Three weeks ago, at Mr.

Nixon's retreat in the Bahamas, we were together. There are two islands, side by side, both owned by Mr. Nixon's friend Bob Abplanalp. One is reserved for the President. On the other is a small resort hotel. I arrived at the President's island as Dan and Kieran were concluding their meeting with him, and when I rejoined Dan at the hotel after dinner I found him surrounded by Kieran, his wife, my wife, and one or two others, Planter's Punch in hand, looking heavenward with a pleased expression on his face, all the more affecting inasmuch as it turned out that he was sound asleep, managing however not to spill a drop from his glass which was propped up in totally reassured equilibrium. He quickly came to in response to my greeting. It was now five days after Jim's victory, a couple of hours after discussing the consequences of it with the President of the United States, and he said to me, "You know, Bill, on the whole, I would say that this has been an above-average week." Eight years ago he had founded the Conservative Party of New York, with Kieran, acting on a suggestion made by *National Review*, which would never have had the organizational machismo to pull it off; from the beginning, it had been their operation; and right now they were feeling pleased. I asked Dan whether the press had accosted him as he came back by helicopter (Marine Force One) to the hotel where we sat, and he said yes, they had indeed, AP, UPI, and the New York *Times*. What had he divulged to them about the meeting? "I merely told them"—he drew on his unlit cigar and aimed his Planter's Punch approximately towards his lips—"that the President informed me that he considers J. Daniel Mahoney the country's most distinguished

American." Next morning, he didn't remember this, and was both relieved—and surprised—that it did not appear in the newspaper accounts of the Conservative invasion of the Bahamas.

Dan wants to discuss one or two points involving personal relations in the Conservative-Republican picture, and one or two others involving the eccentricities of the Securities and Exchange Commission. Then we go downtown together, Jerry driving, with Rowley happily at his side, and we pick up Jim Burnham en route. I ask Jim to read the column I have written analyzing the Coast Guard scandal off Martha's Vineyard, because he will be writing the editorial on the subject for *NR*. My own column homes in on Admiral Bender, who yesterday spoke some nonsense in behalf of the Coast Guard. "Well, says the admiral, you see [I paraphrase], the Russians insisted that the defector, Simas, had stolen $2,000 from the ship's cash fund. No doubt they did say that [I mock]. The question is why the Coast Guard believed it. Would the Coast Guard have believed the Russians if they had said that it had just then been established that Simas was the guy who killed Kirov?" I couldn't remember Kirov's name last night. Jim gives it to me now. "What proof did the Coast Guard demand to see, before believing that poor Simas was a common thief, rather than someone who sought political asylum? And then the admiral went on to say something so mystifying as to achieve absolute inscrutability. You see, he said, Simas greatly prejudiced his case because instead of leaping from the Soviet cutter into the water (as Simas had whispered he was going to do), whence the U.S. Coast

Guard would have plucked him out, Simas leaped from the Soviet boat directly to the American boat, missing the water altogether. Get it? I reasoned that there must be some meaning to this, that perhaps the Geneva Convention has a clause in it assigning to water some sacramental property which transubstantiates a common refugee into a legitimate claimant to political asylum. So I called the greatest lawyer in the world and asked him, and he simply shook his head in dumb amazement. The only relevance I can think of to the Water Version is that maybe the admiral figured that the reason Simas didn't throw himself into the water is that he didn't want to wet those $2,000 he had stolen from the ship's strong box; and therefore, he must have been a common criminal after all."

A few days after writing the column, I heard Mr. Nixon's explanation (to the Advisory Commission) of what had happened: a sleepy State Department type, answering the Coast Guard's question, had consulted the book and replied that it was not the United States Government's policy to "encourage" defectors; which was interpreted by the wretched Coast Guard official in Boston as translatable into permitting the Soviet Navy to seize, torture, shackle, and impound Simas.

I wonder whether, if the transgressing Administration had been Democratic, I and others would have dropped the matter, as indeed it was dropped in a matter of days. There is of course an explanation for that. If you are prepared to believe that the in-guys are presumptively on your side, then you bemoan their delinquencies as you would aberrations, rather than as delinquencies that issue out of their flawed understanding of reality. Thus a

Democratic Administration that signs a conciliatory agreement affecting Laos is presumed to be weakminded, critically short of anti-Communist corpuscles, while a Republican Administration that signs a peace with North Korea is assumed to have got the best deal one can hope to get. *National Review* is increasingly criticized for our softness towards the Nixon Administration, which is sharply contrasted to the unrelenting criticism we leveled against the Eisenhower Administration. The explanation is that with the defeat of Goldwater in 1964 Nixon was the only feasible alternative to a liberal Democrat, and it is the job of conservatives to back what they can reasonably hope to get, even as they continue to burnish the paradigm for us all to keep constantly in mind. The thing about Ike, we explain, is that he took the Republican Party away from Taft, who was strong and knowledgeable and would surely have won the Presidency if he had been nominated. And that he had the power to have done things differently. We could not have said as much, after the Goldwater experience, about a right-wing alternative to Richard Nixon, however enthusiastic we are about Ronald Reagan.

We grind through editorial day, the copy riding up on the dumbwaiter, and down again. Three rings on my buzzer, answered by Priscilla, who rings once, the signal that means she is at her desk, and that the tray is floating down, and that she will distribute the copy to the typists, or to the writers if corrections or amplifications are suggested. On Wednesdays we lunch on sandwiches, briefly, and twenty minutes later are back at work, and the afternoon goes by. Somehow we always manage just to make it in time to take the final line-count, select the paragraphs and editorials that will run, and then at five almost exactly, we have drinks. I say almost at five, because somebody thought to hide the key to the liquor closet in the *Encyclopaedia*, and nobody can remember whether the decision was to stick it in the Booze page of the *EB*, or the Drink page. We are joined by whatever friends of *NR* happen to be in town. The sessions are sometimes routine and uneventful, but sometimes take off, not unusually when catalyzed by Jim McFadden, who is the assistant publisher, in charge of practically everything non-editorial, who is often on, and rouses us from our post-deadline daze with the special vigor of his bonhomie.

Tonight I cannot join them because I must speak at Princeton, so I go off with Rowley. Jerry pulls out, and I raise the glass partition because I will be answering correspondence for the first hour or so of the drive.

There is a two-sentence note from Pat Moynihan, the news being that he has declined Mr. Nixon's invitation to become his ambassador to the United Nations, electing instead, for complicated reasons, to return to Harvard-M.I.T. I had written last week about his proposed appointment. The column was killed in Washington, because a few hours before the release date Moynihan had announced that he wouldn't take the job. But other papers ran it anyway, and Moynihan evidently saw it. I had enjoyed writing the column, knowing Moynihan, however slightly.

I remember insinuating myself down the aisle at Manhattan Center a few days before the election in 1968. It was a great Humphrey-Muskie rally, memorable if only because that was when Ken Galbraith, the ultimate attraction, was stopped dead, as he began to speak, by a young couple who bounded onstage, shed their clothes, and danced about him—or rather the male did, a pig's head in hand, the spectators having just-in-time detained the girl, draping her in a raincoat. The fuzz reached the man a few seconds later, but poor Ken, although he plowed a straight furrow through his hortatory address to the effect that the earth would open up and swallow us all if Nixon was elected, was not able to engage the distracted audience.

But that episode was much later, a dozen speeches featuring the illuminati of the Americans for Democratic Action later. I had arrived as Moynihan was speaking. The audience spotted me, slithering towards the press section, and began to boo. Moynihan paused to reprimand the crowd. "Remember," he said mock-solemnly, "the Church has always made way for late vocations."

A few weeks later, Moynihan's acceptance of a critical position on President-elect Nixon's staff was announced, and a few months after that he telephoned me to say that he wanted personally to explain to *National Review*'s editors the reasons why we should think carefully before rejecting the Family Assistance Plan the President would soon be springing on Congress. He arrived, with two or three aides, for dinner at 73rd, and he spoke evangelistically about a plan he assured us would simultaneously effect humanitarian visions, and satisfy conservative dissatisfactions. Before he left, Tony Dolan and his friend Peter McCann came in. Tony is the right-wing folk singer, a senior at Yale. He had just now taped an exchange on television with SDSer Jim Kunen, author of *The Strawberry Statement*. The two young musicians played for us, Peter McCann sang "Danny Boy" in his special bel canto, and Daniel Patrick Moynihan and his staff left to return to Washington on their military jet, happy with music and wine, if not absolutely reassured about the editors' response to the forthcoming proposal, even though we did promise to take meticulous account of the points he made.

It seemed obvious, with the defeat of the Plan, that Moynihan had either to return to teaching or take a quite different job for Nixon. I felt sorry for Nixon, losing Moynihan as a presence at the White House. Blithe spirits are rare. There was the occasion someone recounted to me, when the formidable Arthur Burns and Patrick, in the Oval Room with the President, were obstinately waiting, one for the other to divulge his version of the proposed welfare budget, whereupon, the impasse being obvious, Moynihan finally said: "All right, Arthur, I'll tell you what. You show me yours, and I'll show you mine." Who will do that kind of thing in the Oval Room, now that Patrick's gone?

To the UN? Not [I wrote] that Mr. Moynihan isn't "qualified" to serve as Ambassador to the UN. He is "qualified" to serve as anything. I remember the old Truth or Consequences game they used to play over the radio, which towards the end was coming up with consequences so extravagant as to satisfy Rabelaisian appetites for the absurd. On one occasion the loser, a mild-mannered middle-aged man, was quickly stripped and dressed in white tie and tails, taken under escort to the stage of Town Hall, a violin stuck in his hand, and catapulted onstage to receive a tumultuous welcome from an overflow house of music lovers who had been tantalized for months in the press about the forthcoming visit of a here-

59

tofore reclusive musical genius from the Thuringian Forest. The poor man lifted his bow to his violin, wooden side to the strings, and the joke was exposed. A practical joke in the grand tradition. If the contestant had been Daniel Patrick Moynihan, I am altogether convinced that even if he had not previously played a single note on the violin, he'd have taken bow to instrument and delivered a perfect concert.

Was Nixon intending a practical joke? I asked. Moynihan has the lowest threshold of crap-tolerance in the civilized world, and the spectacle of Ambassador Moynihan being made to sit in the General Assembly of the United Nations listening to the world's greatest concentration of drivel in four languages is the spectacle of a man who, in the Orwellian situation, is sent to be tortured by just exactly those means that researchers have discovered most acutely pain him. On the other hand, could it be that Mr. Nixon has decided to bust up the joint? Because if so, he has selected just the right man; absolutely no one is better qualified. Moynihan might very well, after the first sentence about colonialism from, say, the Czechoslovakian ambassador, stand up and in a very few minutes make Khrushchev's shoe-pounding episode look like a milestone of decorum. Maybe those are his instructions? They would not need to be very explicit, unless possibly they were that Moynihan, having been appointed, should set a new precedent by never even appearing at the UN, even as Queen Victoria, after Albert's death, managed to govern for so many years without being seen by anyone except her Prime Minister. But that would be a theatrical waste. Probably the best ambassador we could send to the UN, for so long as we adopt a passive role towards it, would be a deaf-mute. Second best, intending a quite contrary attitude, is Daniel Patrick Moynihan. Let us all pray that between now and his investiture he is not given any crash courses in diplomacy. That would ruin his perfect pitch.

Patrick writes me, simply, "Alas, it is not to be. But you certainly made it sound attractive."

The Musical Heritage Society has sent me thirty long-playing records, most of them the cantatas of Bach, with a note expressing thanks for my devotion to music—a euphemism for writing a column advising music lovers of the Beethoven-bargain the Society was offering. I acknowledge the gift most gratefully, and guilt-free, since I cannot believe that any words of mine commending the work of Bach would constitute payola . . . I most strongly urge a dispirited Massachusetts Republican *against* founding a Conservative Party, never mind his complaint that the gentleman who ran against Teddy Kennedy—Josiah Spaulding—was more liberal than Kennedy. And never mind, I reminisce, that Si Spaulding is an old friend. I met him at Yale, as an undergraduate, and he and Jim, freshmen at the Law School, organized a fresh-cider delivery service, one dollar per gallon, and would personally deliver the stuff to your room, carrying a gallon on each finger, eight per person, Horatio Algers IV. Jim was Si's best man, and the maid of honor was Jackie Bouvier . . . irrelevant. I stress to my correspondent that the situation in New York State is unique, that the fact that Massachusetts Republicans came so close to knocking Si out in the primary suggests that the Republican Party remains a viable vehicle for Republican conservatives. (I must write a column on the subject.) David Keene, the

61

bright young lawyer and chairman of Young Americans for Freedom who resigned a few weeks ago in order to go to work for Agnew, has already called to urge that I pour cold water on those who, intoxicated by Jim's extraordinary victory, are dreaming about Conservative Parties in their own states.

I have a very complimentary and therefore very pleasant letter from a professor at the University of Massachusetts, which however I read eagerly for reasons that supplement vanity. "I very much enjoyed your article on Russia in December PLAYBOY. I frequently enjoy your extravagant prose and good humor, fantastical asides and abrupt, serious, Chestertonian decencies. Your pieces are wise and witty. However, very specifically this article intrigued me because of my own visit to Russia. I lived in Finland (your comment on young Finns was uproarious and true) for a year on scholarship to Helsinki University and took advantage of geography to have a Red Christmas, in Leningrad and Moscow. Many of your comments vibrated strings within my own experience and articulated clearly some things I had felt more vaguely."

I have been brooding about the article, which appeared on the newsstands a month ago. It was a long piece, almost ten thousand words, and I had on finishing it a sense of satisfaction I can only remember having taken on the completion of two other pieces I wrote (and one book). I was tempted to *Playboy* because I have become friends with David Butler, the young man who did the endless interview with me published during the spring, and he urged me to write more extensively about my Russian trip than I could do in my columns. So I did, the

piece ran absolutely unchanged, and I sat back in anticipation of the considerable reaction I would get from
Playboy's five and one-half million purchasers, which (we
publishers make it a point of stressing) means as an absolute minimum, double that number of readers. Ten million readers of my views on Russia! Five per cent of the
population of America, 10 per cent of the reading population of America.

The response? This is the *only* letter I received. I get
(someone on the staff once counted) about 600 letters a
week, which sounds like a lot, but I suppose isn't, when
you take into account that people write me a) who are
interested in the cause, b) who think I might prove useful, in some connection or other, c) who read *National
Review*, which has a circulation of about 110,000, d) who
read my newspaper column, which appears in over 300
newspapers, e) who read my occasional articles here and
there, and f) who see my television program, which runs
weekly in a hundred "markets," as we are taught to say.
Still, only *one* letter from *Playboy* readers. David Butler,
who is a gentleman, keeps consoling me by sending on
the few letters that come in from big shots to whom *Playboy* has sent offprints of the article, soliciting reactions,
from which they will distill a letters section. Even these
are not all *that* numerous, and it begins to dawn on me
that all that talent at *Playboy* that is engaged in producing the non-sex part of the magazine—what Garry Wills
calls the "magazine within a magazine"—simply is not
read. That does not mean that it doesn't serve a purpose.
It does: one purpose being psychological, the other commercial.

It helps to persuade the editor-publisher, Mr. Hugh

Hefner, that he is engaged in a serious enterprise, whose success depends on other things than breasts exposed, and pudenda limned (though I note in the December issue that they are no longer veiled). Commercially? It is obviously easier for such advertisers as General Motors to answer complaints against their patronage by citing all the Harvard theologians who have written for *Playboy* during the past year. Like keeping the Bible on the bookshelf of the whorehouse: it is after all there, for those who want it. (Who to write for nowadays, among the big magazines, *Esquire* being out because I have a lawsuit pending against it?) . . . Poor Hefner. There are two stories about him I cherish. He was asked at a press conference a while back: Mr. Hefner, you have a very pretty 17-year-old daughter. Do you intend to make her a Playmate? Stunned silence. Then he speaks, with what I consider the most resourceful answer in the history of people-on-the-spot. No, he says, because it happens that, notwithstanding all my efforts to do something about it, a strain of Puritan blood continues to reside within my system. I *hate* that strain; but I am powerless to neutralize it, though I shall devote my life to the attempt to do so. That is a tough answer, as the kids used to put it until thank God that verbal corruption was spent.

The other episode involves me. It was a 5th Avenue apartment, and the local editor of *Paris-Match* was entertaining the boss from Paris and one or two friends. After dinner the host said, Look, if you don't mind, I'd like to watch a television program that's about to go on, pitting Buckley against Hefner, because it ought to be quite a show [it wasn't], and he explained to his acquiescent guests who I was, and they turned on the set. Inexplicably, the picture came on but the sound did not, until after four or five minutes, when finally the marginal twiddle with the dial brought it on, and the Frenchmen after a second or two winced with surprise because, studying the speechless visages of the principals, they had all tacitly come to the conclusion that I was Hefner, and Hefner was I; he being, in their reading of our faces, clearly the conservative ascetic, I the freeliver . . .

Hefner is known to be an eccentric, and he is of course. Also, when you are in his company, he is a man of extraordinary courtesy, who once took me painstakingly room-after-room through his exhaustingly depressing palace in Chicago, Pepsi-Cola in hand (we were panelists for an NBC program on vice, waiting for the crew to set up), and later on sent me to the airport in his quite extraordinary limousine, after carefully instructing me on how to use the car's telephone . . . How much harm does *Playboy* do in fact, I have often asked myself, never getting much further than the presumptive disapproval of it, which I extend to any publication,—or person—that declines to accept extra-personal or extra-positivist norms. Then too the pathetic tastelessness. Like at Christmastime I receive a letter. It is obviously a form letter, with the "Dear Bill" typed in with typeface that almost but not quite looks like the rest of the letter. And it is signed not with a signature, faked or otherwise, but by the printed-typed names,

> Hugh M. Hefner
> A. C. Spectorsky
> and The Editors
> of PLAYBOY.

A Christmas check!

65

How to reply, and *not* hurt his feelings. I can understand the occasional necessity to execute people, but never to hurt their feelings, which by the way I consider to be the principal reason why many husbands and wives do not separate. I wrote, finally, "Dear Hugh: You are very generous and very thoughtful, but you see, I precisely do *not* desire to be a 'member of the *Playboy* family.' I write for you, occasionally, because I wish to reach your audience, and I do so in spite of my foreboding that there are, inevitably, those who will believe I have become a natural son of *Playboy*. Pray do not misunderstand me. I am happy to be your friend, if you desire me to be, and extremely happy to have become the friend of your associate David Butler. But friendly to your enterprise, by no means. I return the check, again with my thanks. Keep it, or turn it over to any local organization engaged in comstockery. Yours cordially." . . . I do not think there is any obvious reason to write again for *Playboy*, but I do not doubt that Hugh (those who know him well call him Hef) will ask me to do so, because he accepts misunderstanding, and even abuse, as a part of his tribulation, and who knows it may provide him with a sense of mission; who knows? We are nearing Princeton.

My habit is to read my portfolio, containing the correspondence that led to my speech, as late as possible. The advantages are negative and positive. It means that you are *not* reminded, say at the beginning of a week during which you must speak four or five times, of the awful gauntlet you will need to run before reaching Stamford for the weekend. And it means that you will remember more easily what are the special circumstances of the

66

immediate engagement—in Princeton's case, that the principal character is a young man, obviously of great entrepreneurial resourcefulness, who is not affiliated with student government, or with the formal lecture series, who has his own organization (Undergraduates for a Stable America, this one is called) and who actually went out and raised the money to pay the fee, and that isn't easy. The great majority of the colleges that invite you have no trouble with the money. It is there, taken from the student fees that are exacted at the beginning of every year. It is at places like Harvard, Yale, and Princeton that lecturers run into difficulty, because these colleges are not accustomed to paying their speakers the commercial rate; and speakers tend to indulge them, in part out of tradition, in part out of a curiosity to have a look at what used to be the redoubts of social and intellectual patricians. (They aren't that any longer, we all know, but they are getting as long a run as possible from their reputation.) I have spoken, I reflect, six times at Princeton: once to the Whig-Clio Association, for a perfunctory fee; four times to the Graduate School, for no fee at all; and once for a slightly better than perfunctory fee, at a great brawl, a panel at which Arthur Schlesinger and Richard Rovere also spoke, Eric Goldman presiding: an unhappy memory, because we did not get anywhere.

I have with me a black folder, and in it I have seven speeches, three of which are current and last about 45 minutes each. Of these three, I composed one three years ago, the second two years ago, the third this spring. Nowadays when I am asked for the topic of my lecture, my agent says always the same thing, "Reflections on the Current Disorder." I can run any one of my three speeches under that title; and anyway, nobody ever cares what title you give your speech. I have been having trouble with my Number Three speech (the most current), and am unhappy about it. It must be that it is over-analytical, and contains too many quotations from people like Jefferson and Hamilton—"and other racists," as one student will complain, tomorrow, at Bridgeport. I do not like to give extemporaneous speeches, or even to speak only from notes, because I discovered years ago that my performances are too erratic. I traveled to a debate at Madison, Wisconsin, with Norman Cousins a decade ago (we would take opposite sides on the proposed suspension of nuclear testing), and he told me that he began his lecture career from a full text, traveled through notes-only, down to one 3 x 5 card; and now he uses nothing at all. During approximately the same period, I have traveled in exactly the opposite direction, and that is notwithstanding a natural glibness. I remember a few years ago, at the University of Washington, a questioner who, having heard my answer to some question or other, rose again, this time to protest that I had anticipated his question and read my answer from a prepared text, requiring me to lift all the papers from the podium and deposit them ceremoniously at the chairman's table, to prove that I was not cheating during my exam. On the other hand I am incapable of memorizing. One of the speeches in my black binder I have delivered maybe fifty times, and I could not recite from memory two consecutive sentences from it. I do not know why my memory is so bad, or for that matter why I read so slowly. Isabel Paterson was able to tell me why, even as she knew how to crack *all* the riddles of the universe, in the well-tempered and irascible prose that made her, for so many years, the principal attraction of the *Herald Tribune* Book Review. She wrote me that my two difficulties had the same cause, namely that I had been taught too late how to read, the right age being three, or four at the latest, whereas I was illiterate until six or seven. Who knows, she may be right.

I scribble a note or two, attempting an introduction that will take into account the situation as I can deduce it from the correspondence of young Harding Jones, the conservative huckster who, at age 19 (how *do* they do it?), appears to be managing an extraordinary share of the major events at Princeton University. We approach the appointed building, and I draw a deep breath, fumble finally with my clipboard, inserting everything there I might conceivably need. The next five hours (it averages five hours at colleges) will be exacting, but whenever I veer towards self-pity I think of the extreme on one side: the matador, say, who does not know confidently that he will survive his performance (although the odds are with him). But then, because I also loathe the opposite of self-pity, I think of musicians. How wonderful to make one's living by playing music. Granted the drudgery of scales and arpeggios, when Rosalyn Tureck goes to Carnegie Hall she is first greeted not by the promoters, or the trustees, or the president of Carnegie Hall Inc., or by apprentice pianists; but by the audience. A bow, and she sits down, fusses with the bench, dabs the handkerchief on her palm, brings her hands down slowly, and then begins: what, to be sure, she may have played before ten times fifty times, but does

69

one get *tired* of hearing the music one plays, as a lecturer gets tired of hearing again a speech he has delivered so often? Inconceivable.

There are maybe two hundred people crowding the room. I am given sherry, and introduced to them. They approach me, and the astonishing Mr. Jones knows almost all of them by name, managing even to whisper to me, in some cases, the salient point about the boy, or the girl, or the professor, he is about to introduce me to. Harding *does not like it* when I tarry too long with one person, which of course I would not do if by so doing it looked as if I were holding up the line, but since the line at college functions of this sort is spontaneous and amorphous (one part natural courtesy; one the unwillingness of the student to appear as though his desire to meet you, at best a velleity, justifies the indignity of standing in line, which you do only to buy a ticket for The Grateful Dead, and even then, only because you promised to take your girl), it easily decomposes, if you should happen to pause overlong to talk to someone. I listen hard, and though there isn't much cross-talk that is investigatory in nature, there is an awful lot of the kind of thing that needs parrying. Not many Mr.-Buckley-why-do-you-oppose-the-Family-Assistance-Plan? but quite a few Mr.-Buckley-*how*-can-you-defend-Agnew? There is absolutely no net impression that distinguishes Princeton. The girls are pretty and ugly, the boys shy and extrovert, the faculty distant and warm. There is no Incident; there very seldom is. The Incident-Makers either stay away, most of them, or else they decide, on these occasions, simply to observe, and to play the game. Mostly, the Incident-Makers prefer anonymous, institutional confrontations, and I think that that is an uncelebrated datum.

. . . Last June I sat preparing to deliver the Commencement Address at the University of California at Riverside, while the black student president went on and on and on, in his address preceding my own, about wars fascism and imperialism. And then, while I was being introduced by the chancellor, two students approached and presented me with a live pig. Cheers and applause came from a hundred or so students, out of three or four thousand in the crowd. After it was all over, the student body president approached me, with a wonderful combination of diffidence and bumptiousness, to say that he disapproved of the pig-bit, but that I was not to mistake this for approval of *anything* I had said, presumably not even the passage in my speech in which I deplored race prejudice.

Two weeks ago, in St. Paul, a young assistant to the rabbi at whose synagogue I had just finished speaking was asked in the crush in the hall as we were dispersing, did he want to meet me, to which he whispered hell no, even as the gentleman on my left, unaware of the reply, propelled me towards him, so that, perforce, we shook hands. "Congratulations," he said grimly. "You certainly succeeded in snowing the audience." "How?" I asked. "Well, for instance, by saying that we aren't spending a greater percentage of our gross national product on the military than we were under Truman, when in fact the important thing is that in absolute terms we are spending maybe three times as much." I answered with the measured, sleep-inducing matter-of-factness that is useful in defusing tense situations, as if I had not heard the words

71

he uttered to the rabbi, but the exchange was lost in the general bustle. As we drove away my host, a doctor, one of the types from whose view nothing escapes, lightly probed me, and of course I told him the truth, that I had heard it all. He apologized for the social dislocation, and explained that the young man's father was a legislator in the New York Assembly, who last April reversed himself and cast the deciding vote to relax the abortion law, in punishment for which he had failed of re-election, and the son was for that reason overwrought, particularly against conservative Catholics, but that he, the doctor, speaking for the rabbi and all the sponsors of the event, was nevertheless appalled by the boy's rudeness. I dismissed it as utterly inconsequential, totally understandable, infinitely excusable, etc., etc., even though the sting punctured, and one of these days I will perhaps know enough about myself, though I do not spend much time in conscious introspection—this journal being a spectacular exception—to know whether such hurts are an offense pure and simple against my vanity, or whether, as I would prefer to think, they offend me as ruptures of the membrane of social affections (Garry Wills's term) that makes it possible for people to live together, people by definition being people who disagree on questions trivial and substantial.

There is none of that at the reception at Princeton, and finally I am led into a very large dining room, the tables splendidly appointed for the hundred insiders involved in the evening's enterprise, and I am seated, Harding on my left, a confederate of his on my right, and to *his* right, the President of Princeton University, Mr. Goheen, whose hand I shook at the reception, won-

72

dering even then what had got *him* there, putting down his appearance as another tribute to Harding's manipulative genius. But *dinner?* (I cannot imagine a college president going out for dinner, except as a matter of duty.) I looked over the other diners, and deduced that the portlier members, sprinkled among the boys and girls, were: Influential Alumni. During the whole of dinner I am engaged in conversation left and right, and do not exchange a word with President Goheen, which begins to strike me as a little unnatural, but it isn't easy to do something about it, i.e., to lean over the student situated between us; and anyway, I also begin to wonder whether the president would not just as soon have it that way. Harding, as the meat is being served, asked would I mind saying just a *few* words to the dinner guests before we go on to the auditorium, to which of course the only answer you can make, unless you are Evelyn Waugh or Edmund Wilson, is well, okay, and a sharp host will interpret, by the length of time you spend slurring the word "well," just how disconcertedly you accept the call to extra duty. Then you get down to thinking.

One of my disabilities is that I cannot think at all without a pen in my hand, and a sheet of paper in front of me; any pen, any paper. Or, if I am being questioned, or grilled; then I can think . . . Willmoore Kendall, the finest teacher I knew at Yale, the most difficult human being I have ever known, at Yale or elsewhere, found himself during one summer in the course of his eccentric career ferrying building materials from Washington, D.C., where he was temporarily working for a think-tank, to New Haven, where he was building a house on property he owned adjacent to the property of his old

73

friend Cleanth Brooks, with whom he was on speaking terms in odd months of the year, or in even years—I forget; Willmoore's calendar was inscrutable, the only givens being that he must not be on speaking terms with more than three people at any one time. I asked him one night—he often paused at Stamford—how was it worth his time himself to drive two or three times a week in his jeep station wagon over so long a distance, merely to save the freight, which after all was not that expensive; and he replied that whatever he was engaged in, even driving a jeep station wagon, he was also *thinking*, and that he found it just as easy to *think* while turning the wheel of an automobile and applying pressure to the pedals as while sitting in his study. And indeed, when he was ready to write, he would do so in the fabled manner of those who simply transcribe what their thought has worked up for them, down to the dotted i's. John C. Calhoun, we are told, used to like to plow his farm because after doing so he could then sit down and write out, as quickly as he could move his pen, the speech or essay that his thoughts had constructed for him.

Think, then—I grab my clipboard, and brandish my pen. One tries to think first, in such a situation, of a funny story or two that are appropriate to the occasion. I have one for the speaker-who-has-just-been-asked-to-speak-unprepared. It never fails, and if the priest who in due course will give me extreme unction should happen to ask me if I have anything I wish to say, I shall regale him with that same funny story. After that, if possible, recount something that relates to the local situation. Well, here I am, separated from Mr. Goheen, and the students must have thought about that, and I recall the vexations I and my associates encountered on the *Yale Daily News,* having organized our annual dinner around the retirement of the then-President of Yale, Charles Seymour. I had extended invitations to all the presidents of the Ivy League Colleges, and got acceptances from all of them (a careful operation: first we got General Eisenhower of Columbia to accept, and that way we could say to James Conant of Harvard: General Eisenhower has already accepted . . .). The matter of seating arose, and we decided that the presidents should fan out from the center of the table, beginning with the man who had the longest tenure, which suggested a line beginning with Conant, and ending with Stassen of Pennsylvania. All very well and good until we consulted *Who's Who* and discovered that both Conant *and* Dodds of Princeton listed June 1933 as the date of their election to the presidency of their universities. I called a 19-year-old heeler, which is what they call the servile class at Yale who are competing for election to one of the extra-curricular organizations, and gave him the task of discovering what *day* in June Conant and Dodds had been elected. He came back what seemed like weeks later, hollow-eyed, to report that it was very complicated. Conant had been elected one week, by one of Harvard's two governing bodies (subject to ratification by the second body, two weeks later). One week later (you guessed it), Dodds was named by Princeton's *only* governing body. I asked the heeler whether the acquiescence of the second of Harvard's governing bodies was by tradition automatic—in which case we could assume that the first election was authoritative. But the question made him cry. So we decided to assume it was so, and put Conant first . . . Well, that story would be

75

good for a minute or two. The boys would obviously like me to tease Goheen a bit, since they are conservative, and he is liberal, so I thank him for endorsing the Princeton Plan, according to which students were let out during the two weeks before election, that they might have themselves a little participatory democracy. The categorical assumption was that they would proceed, a body militant, to be Clean for Gene or whoever was that season's cutting edge for liberalism. I announce that the psephologists have just completed a study that reveals that the participation of Princeton volunteers was the very thing that brought my brother over the edge to victory. The boys love that, and Mr. Goheen smiles, rather like St. Sebastian at the executioner.

Probably not more than four minutes, and you cannot get away with much less than that, particularly when you see that in anticipation, the audience has moved back their chairs, the older members of it lighting up their cigars.

The formal dinner breaks up, a few minutes of questions, during which I try to grope my way toward Mr. Goheen, whom I feel at this point I am coming close to seriously neglecting, but a graduate student wants to know about something *National Review* said and shouldn't have said in the current issue, or else something *National Review* didn't say but should have said. I ask Harding if he can fetch me up a brandy, which miraculously he does, so that when we march off to the abattoir, I am in a moderate state of equilibrium.

I have decided to give my Number Three speech, though it is a little bit difficult, and as I am being introduced I wonder how I might communicate this to the audience, so that it will not be too disappointed, after the initial roll, at being made to listen to something other than the Ride of the Valkyries—and so, after the pleasantries, I find myself saying that what I will proceed to say is historical and analytical, but that it will repay the close attention of the audience, whether right- or left-minded, because the speech is "exquisitely wrought." The reaction is sharply interesting, because it brings howls of both appreciative and derisive laughter, followed—or am I imagining it?—by a quite preternatural silence which is not broken during the ensuing 45 minutes.

"I have been following your career closely for the past several years," I will hear from a stranger a few days later, "and believe that I have never seen an article that was as unfair to you as the enclosed, which should make it some sort of collector's item. It is from the December 4 copy of the *Trentonian*, one of the two daily newspapers that service (?) Trenton, N.J." How unfair is it, I wonder after reading it . . .

PRINCETON—The small band of campus conservatives at Princeton University assembled at Dillon Gym Wednesday night to see and hear the man they call "The Godfather." For the conservatives, the event took on the quality of a ritualistic reaffirmation of the faith. Many arrived with dates for the big event, dressed to the nines as if for the junior prom, walking ostentatiously down the long center aisle to the section of seats at the front of the gym

77

closest to the great man and marked off with orange-and-black crepe paper ribbons and signs saying "Reserved."

It takes guts to be a conservative at Princeton University. If you are one you've got to flaunt it, to show machismo like a member of a street gang walking through alien turf. But the conservatives who came to experience William F. Buckley Jr. were outnumbered perhaps 10 to one by the liberals and radicals who came for other reasons—perhaps to be shocked or outraged or entertained. Buckley was not shocking or outrageous. The sneering enfant terrible of the right who wrote "God and Man at Yale" is no more. Buckley cannot yet manage a real smile (the closest he gets to one is a convulsive baring of his upper teeth) but nonetheless he has mellowed.

Nor is Buckley, to a generation reared on a diet of television images, very entertaining. William F. Buckley isn't a politician, although he has run for office; he isn't a political philosopher, although he writes political philosophy; he isn't really a journalist, although he has spent his whole adult life editing a journal. He is essentially an artist of language practicing his art for its own sake. His speeches are not really speeches but tours de force of workmanship, labored over with a gem-cutter's skill and patience and then fastidiously laid before a dazzled audience.

The theme of Buckley's exercise Wednesday night was essentially simple: each man's freedom extends only so far as it can extend without impinging on another man's; hence no rights can be absolute;

hence there are occasions when, for the sake of freedom, government must repress certain actions that tend to destroy freedom.

The audience seized on the word "repression," the campus trigger-word that, by a simple mention, starts the liberal saliva dripping in the best Pavlovian manner.

Buckley was talking about the rule of law. What most of his listeners thought he was talking about was law-'n-order. The difference between the concepts is the difference between Aristotle and his fellow-countryman who presently is in possession of the vice-presidency. The blame for the audience's confusion lay with Buckley. He is an anachronism. In an era when television images are comfortingly soft-edged, his language is disturbingly precise, hard and crystalline. Television demands that you sit back and let your mind be massaged; Buckley demands that you lean forward and listen and think.

He makes no concessions to weaknesses of his hearers. He read through his speech at a rapid, steady pace despite all distractions—dogs wandering in front of the podium, applause, hisses, cheers. [Wrong. The crowd was silent.] In the middle of his conclusion the microphone went dead but Buckley went implacably on [what was the alternative?] although the last two minutes of the speech were inaudible to anyone more than 30 feet away. The young people in Dillon Gym, when they realized the speech was over, seemed momentarily bewildered. They knew Buckley had done something dazzling and unusual, but they seemed not sure how they were to react to it. Finally most of them faked it by simultaneously clapping loudly and looking thoughtful.

The Daily Princetonian's story by contrast referred to my " 'gloomy' and complex examination of historical attitudes towards repression," and said of the address that it was "received with respect and restraint."

. . . The question period is lively, but when it is over, I have the feeling that it is over to almost everyone's relief; and I speed away to a small reception at Eric Goldman's house, to which he permitted me to invite a nephew-godson-sophomore—a graceful young man who however says not a word—and the assistant headmaster of my old preparatory school (and his wife), retired now and working for the Board of Admissions at Princeton. Brock Brower, the journalist, is there, and there is animated conversation for almost an hour, after which I leave, get into the car, and fuss again with correspondence. Pat is asleep when I get to 73rd, the television on; I turn it off quietly, which always wakes her up, and causes her to demand to know why I thought she was asleep, when in fact she was listening intensely. But before the tirade is half done, she is back asleep, consummating an exercise that begins when she turns *on* the television, which she does when she is ready to go to sleep.

THURSDAY. I am on the road early, because I must be at the University of Bridgeport by 11 A.M., for a debate with Dick Gregory. I am concerned that Rowley's walker won't return him in time; but she does, and he goes straightaway, excitedly, into the car. Bill (the driver who alternates with Jerry) has brought the mail from the office, and I resolve to work on it until we reach Westport, which will give me fifteen minutes to think about Dick Gregory.

I wrote last week that there might well be imperative military reasons for the bombing strike in North Vietnam, and that certainly there had been no breach in our truce terms, inasmuch as the enemy's going to the negotiating table at Paris had not amounted, after thirty months, to anything more than their going to the negotiating table at Paris. "Dear Sir: You're not only a wordmonger but a warmonger as well. Only a totally insane person would recommend a continuation of the bombing and murdering of the N. Vietnamese, and I know you're not insane because you can use multi-syllable words. Why do you want to kill humans??? Sincerely, . . ." I should *hope* sincerely. I scratch "na" on the letter, which means "not answered," and happens to only about 10 per cent of my mail. That was from Detroit . . . From Riverdale, New York, "Dear Sir: That people even bother listening to you only proves that what most politicians use as a credo, 'The Masses are the Asses' is well founded. To me—every time you open your mouth it seems only shit comes out of it which confirms what one of our teachers said, 'You mean Buckley, he is full of *shit!*' Judging from your eye movements we are certain you must be a 'Psycho.' Good reason Yale didn't want you on their board. And now, your brother, the phoney is also in the act." And the signature, no closing. na . . . Then there is someone who oscillates from sarcasm to dissimulation. You would think he had tipped his hand conclusively by beginning his letter, "Dear Mr. Puke-ley." But no, he switches mood right away: "I do so agree with you; *brains aren't everything;* those intellectuals always turn out to be no-good, socialist types. I like red-blooded Americans like you who"—now, back we go into the first mode—"work for a living with their *hands,* not their brains. The Republican party needs men like you and Spirew [thus] Agnew, who calls a spade a spade. And Mrs. Mitchell is great, too." He cannot think how to weave a crack into these two references, and is apparently satisfied that the mere mention of their names is enough. "We hate the Right things: Spics, jews, Commie Spics, and dirty niggers. I read every word you write; God bless you. God bless you, and Nixon. Your friend," a signature, but no address. He probably saw the movie *Joe,* and thought the letter a reenactment.

But then an altogether anonymous letter, no name *or* address, but overflowing with gutsy solidarity with me. "Dear Bill: On behalf of your brother and in regard to Mr. Pete Hamill the following message was shot off . . . It could be captioned 'The Wearing o' the Green.' 'Dear Pete: Read your charming article about Jim Buckley, the Castle Irishman. The next time you see an Irish-looking guy with grass stains around his mouth, I want you to know he's not starving to death because of Buckley and the Castle Irishmen; he's working up a load so that he can projectile it into your lousy, Irish face. (s) Erin Go Bragh.' " God. Pete Hamill wrote vigorously against Jim during the campaign, cranking up the explanation that the Buckleys were "Castle Irishmen," a term I had not heard before except when it was used by Hamill to describe me, after I wrote, for *Esquire*, a piece on Truman Capote's famous party a few years ago.

"Pete Hamill [I had written] reviewed the affair most awfully sociologically, from his desk at the New York *Post* (from where else?). The device was to contrive wisps of frivolous conversation, à la *The Women*, and juxtapose them with horror stories from the Vietnamese battlefront (get it?), so as to effect a Stendhalian contrast that would Arouse the Conscience of Versailles. [I gave examples.] . . . The demonstration was on the order of subtlety of (Carl Foreman's) *The Victors'*, in which, just in case you are under the impression that war is a game of soccer at Eton, he sets up an execution of an American deserter (must have been Private Slovik, since he was the only one) during the Second World War, with music blaring out of an adjacent **PX**, 'Have yourself a merry little Christmas/Through the years we all will be together . . .' The implicit point . . . being that one shouldn't enjoy oneself publicly while there is a war on, and of course such advice would be easier to accept from an evangelist of continence who less visibly than Mr. Hamill enjoys weaving the luridities of Vietnam through his editorial loom. But it is true that certain functionaries intimately involved in the Vietnam War deemed it inappropriate to frug-with-Kay [Graham] at Truman's blast; indeed, that was just the reason why Secretary McNamara did not come; at least, that is the reason he gave to Truman Capote for, regretfully, declining his kind invitation. But he was one of few who did decline and the only one on record to have given that reason for declining, and he did not, Mr. Capote informs us, make that point censoriously. After all, one of the reasons why there is fighting in Vietnam is so that people can have fun together back home. And besides, if society accepted the dictum that so long as some people are suffering, others may not party together, there would never be any partying at all, especially not on the evening of Mr. Capote's ball, when the agony experienced by some of the uninvited almost certainly exceeded that of the calm and resolute young men in Vietnam, who, if polled, would, almost surely, produce much more contempt for Pete Hamill than for Truman Capote."

I have gradually come to know that when you write that way about people you make very tenacious enemies, and sure enough, during the campaign Hamill was saying things on the order of, "Buckley [J., though one must suppose, a fortiori, W.] is against everything that has made life in this country an acceptable condition for working people." And, "Buckley is a patronizing agent of the upper class, slumming with the common folk, and if they elect him, they will get the betrayal they deserve." And on and *on* about the Castle Irish, which if we take Hamill's word for it, is what they called the quisling-types who, siding with the English, were pleased to betray their freedom-seeking countrymen, in order to gobble the social scraps vouchsafed them from the Castle whence the English tyrannized the Irish people. I dropped Hamill a note several years ago, I remember, praising a column he had written on the books he had read during the year. What is the point in denying his *talent?* I was not engaged in guile. I have *never* understood the point in disparaging the *skills* of your adversaries. That sort of thing shouldn't go beyond Virginia

84

Kirkus and the Donald Duck School of literary criticism, or at the other end, John Birch. I wonder. If I *hadn't* hit him so hard about the Capote ball (he resented the attack in print, at the time), would he have weighed in as hysterically against Jim? On the other hand, it wasn't Hamill, but the New York *Times*, that said (in an editorial) that Goodell's was "the voice of a public official determined to keep freedom from being assassinated by the ruthless nightriders of the political right." (What an *embarrassment* the *Times'* editorials are to so many of the *Times'* reporters, and executives: I described them once as Cotton Mather rewriting Eleanor Roosevelt, and the appreciation from a *Times* writer, on the road with my brother, was very nearly hysterical with released pleasure, like the nun who cannot contain herself on hearing a ribald truth spoken about the mother superior.)

And then, too, I never did anything to Harriet Van Horne (pure neglect), and *she* said, "If this election goes as President Nixon would like it to go, the long trail will soon be entering a dark tunnel . . ." (At the pre-election rally in Queens, I "appealed" to the "higher intelligence of Harriet Van Horne: How can nightriders live in tunnels? Really, the voices of moderation ought to concert their metaphors. If you think it's easy to have *one* foot in the tunnel, and the *other* foot in the stirrup of a horse . . ." The crowds love that sort of thing. So do I.) . . . But the best would come the day *after* Jim's election, by Robert Mayer, in *Newsday*: "It crept in during the night. It was hanging over the city when we awoke yesterday, gray and imponderable, like the fog. Morning became afternoon and still it would not go away, the shame, the bur-

85

den, the thorny crown of collective guilt. We sat in darkened apartments, Dostoyevskyan, vaguely aware of gray light filtering in through the windows, unable to stir outside, unwilling to face our neighbors, eyes cast down, unseeing. New York! New York had come to this . . ."

At the 15th Anniversary party for *National Review,* held three weeks ago at the Tavern on the Green, I amused myself by quoting this passage to the guests, in the presence of my lamb-like brother, who had brought on the shame of New York. A week later I heard from the author's publisher, William Attwood, who had been ambassador to Guinea (as published in *NR,* slightly edited at his request):

Dear Bill:

Many thanks for not including me in your Central Park celebration of NATIONAL REVIEW's Fifteenth Anniversary. Your public readings from *Newsday* etc. on the doleful meaning to the Republic of the election of your brother, as reported by Israel Shenker of the *Times,* might have compelled me to stalk out with whatever dignity I could muster —something I have not done since the opening of a Mongolian cultural exhibition in Conakry in 1963. After the usual expressions of eternal friendship (based on long-standing cultural cooperation) between the Guinean and Mongolian peoples, the orators digressed into a denunciation of genocide and other international torts and misdeeds being committed by your ambassador's then employers. Since the only refreshments available were Mainland Chinese brandy and local (nationalized) soda pop, I

86

had been hoping for a pretext to get away—which I'm sure would not have been the case at your party.

My invitation to you to visit your major Long Island outlet at any time of your choosing still stands. Parts of our building look as if they had been designed by a family of moles, but I will have a bar and dining room in operation by January, with a private entrance for controversial personalities. Yours,

The party itself was a great, relaxed success, the tone of it having been set by invitations which were austerely formal on the front side, requesting the pleasure of the recipient's "presence at a"—and then on the overside, "PERFECTLY SMASHINGLY ABSOLUTELY WILD KNOCK-DOWN DRAG-OUT NO HOLDS BARRED GREAT BIG NOISY UNINHIBITED BRAWL OF A P*A*R*T*Y." The Dixieland music was by Wild Bill Davison, the rock by Peter McCann's group, The Repairs, most of them students at Fairfield and Yale. I had arranged for a surprise: the great Rosalyn Tureck had agreed to come and play for six or seven minutes. We agreed that that was about as much serious music as 500 party-goers could take in in total appreciative concentration. She would do the *Chromatic Fantasia*, the 29th Variation from the *Goldberg*, and finally the Gigue from the B-flat Partita. At 6 P.M. on the evening of the party, I received word that Rosalyn was in bed with stomach flu. I called my television producer, Warren Steibel, who knows the musical agencies, and he called Columbia Artists who told him that the big-name pianists were out of town, but recommended a young man, Samuel Lipman. It was agreed that Mr. Lipman would telephone me, which he did five minutes later. He sounded wonderfully

87

amiable. I felt it prudent to describe carefully the circumstances, and was happy to learn that he was a reader of *National Review*, less happy to learn that he had an advanced degree in political science from Berkeley. He did not have in his repertory the music I particularly wanted, but, strong on Rachmaninoff, he proposed that I listen to a couple of little-known preludes and, putting his telephone receiver down, he proceeded to play bits and pieces from them. I thought them neither familiar enough for the purpose nor attention-getting enough, and asked him if he had any Bach ready to go; he said yes, the E-minor Toccata, the theme of which, to remind me, he quickly rattled off on the piano, and we agreed he would finish with the supreme chestnut, the C-sharp-minor Prelude of Rachmaninoff. He reminded me that it ends very quietly, whereas a bang-bang ending is preferable in this kind of situation, but he agreed that familiarity with the music would make up for the down-beat ending; and it came off very well, without any mutinous noises at all, and no Virgil-Fox hamming up, either.

I have a distinct feeling, reconstructing it all, that Richard Nixon intended to come to the party. I had perfunctorily invited him, as one would expect, and he had not replied, as one would not expect. Then, a week or so before the party, someone from the White House called to confirm the exact place and time. We deduced that it was for the purposes of sending directly there a congratulatory message, and were therefore somewhat surprised to receive such a message the next day, several days ahead of the party, addressed to me not at the Tavern on the Green, but at *National Review*. The following day de Gaulle died, and Nixon sped off to Paris for the funeral, which was held the morning of our party. At about noon, on the day of the party, another call from the White House, asking whether I would like it if the President were to telephone his greetings to the gathering from Air Force One, en route back from Paris, assuming it proved practicable. Of course, I said, we should like that very much, and the White House took on the job of instructing the New York Telephone Company (I assume *that* telephone call was assigned to a *Democratic* civil servant) on how to wire the Tavern on the Green in such a way as to make it absolutely certain that the Presidential voice would come in loud and clear. Then, at about seven, the WH called again, this time to advise that Air Force One had left Orly too late, but that a telegraphed greeting would be delivered in time for the festivities—which made the *second* Presidential greeting, but we didn't reveal *that*. The message was once again warm, and nonperfunctory, and included the tantalizing phrase "I regret that my unforeseen absence from the country prevents me from taking a more personal part in your celebration . . ." A second telegram came in, from Mr. Agnew, and we felt terribly official and appreciated.

A surprise of a different order came a week or two later. The Advisory Commission was meeting with Mr. Nixon in the Oval Office, and the President told the chairman, Dr. Frank Stanton, the president of CBS, that he might find it amusing to hear a couple of sentences from the morning's compilation of news as specially prepared for him every day by his staff; and Mr. Nixon proceeded to read a favorable account of CBS's favorable handling of the Presidential message on inflation. Then, turning to me, Mr. Nixon said I might be interested to know that

89

the entire feature section of that morning's report was devoted to the 15th Anniversary issue of *National Review*, whose importance the staff judged sufficient to warrant appending the full texts of its major articles directly after the paraphrase done for busy Presidents. Mr. Nixon, expansive, asked us if we would like copies of the material he had cited. He pushed a button causing the instant materialization of an aide, whom he directed to have xeroxed and sent the whole of that morning's report to each of the five commissioners. I was greatly surprised, because much can be made of the explicit and inexplicit mannerisms of an eyes-only report prepared for the President, and on the way out Frank Stanton and I predicted to each other that the staff would later prevail on Mr. Nixon to simply forget to send on the briefs; but they did arrive.

The 15th Anniversary issue was done on the theme; "After Liberalism, What?" We invited first a Marxist revolutionary, Professor Eugene Genovese, the same whose ouster from Rutgers University Nixon had joined in urging a few years back—unsuccessfully (i.e., the Democratic governor who said he would *not* fire him beat the Republican challenger who said that if elected he *would* fire him). Genovese is now head of the Department of History at the University of Rochester, and in this article, appearing in such alien surroundings, he poked about the corpse of liberalism with considerable fun, but went on to tell why he is not optimistic about a meaningful swing to the left in this country in this decade. Professor Charles Frankel agreed to uphold the viability of American liberalism, and asked some tough questions, among them whether conservatives are really

90

disposed to do without the *forms* of liberalism, raising the question, Are the forms of liberalism exclusively inherent in liberalism: or are they detachable from it?

Jeffrey Hart argued that the adversary relationship that has developed between America's culture and America's intellectuals is altogether unique in the experience of modern civilization. He explored the roots of that antagonism, and drew pessimistic conclusions. James Burnham asked: Can self-government survive? What happens when the people, and in particular the thought-leaders of the people, fail to exhibit that self-denying restraint without which democratic government simply does not work? He put it that the problem is to achieve "authoritative government which is not authoritarian." But how is *that* done in the absence of an appropriate set of attitudes, which are the vertebrae of functioning societies? His conclusion—no, it isn't that exactly, *the destination of his argument*—leaves one peering into a dark and dense forest which, if we are to make it habitable, would require the recolonization of America.

My own summary was brief, "a very few words." That the best of the troubled youth of today, who for instance most recently discovered Charles Reich in *The Greening of America*, ought to get around to discovering that for many years conservatives have been plugging for the best of what *they*, the Reichians, want, and have been holding up the torch they now gather around so excitedly from the time, permit the expression, they were babies.

It was obvious to the conservatives who grouped together after the Second World War that the centripetalization of power simply had to be arrested. Had to stop for one thing because it threatened to suck all social energy into Washington, leaving the individual in ineffective control over his own destiny. And had to stop as a practical matter, because of the limits of corporate efficiency. It was fourteen years after *NR* began that Peter Drucker would write in *The Age of Discontinuity* that the only thing government can do effectively is wage war and inflate the currency. The special idealism of the youth who went to college or completed college during the postwar years seized on collective fancies—the orthodox socialism of the Henry Wallace campaign, the satellization of which by the Communist Party brought widespread disillusion. And, for a brief season, the dreams of World Federalism. When these fell apart, they fell back to the paunchy liberalism of the fifties, dressed up by the belletristic politics of Adlai Stevenson. The end came in Dallas. It fell to Lyndon Johnson to be the personal victim of the end of that very long hallucination which John Kennedy was never exposed to: the jostling that would come when the highway turned to dirt and potholes, and the public began to realize that no free people could lead happy or full lives by buying one share each of common stock in—The State.

Along came the prophets of quite the other direction. The solipsists. Jack Kerouac, on the road, refusing even to *read* the daily newspapers. The hippies (whom he later reviled) adopted his life-style, without the motion motion motion that was the operative narcotic during Kerouac's period—stressing instead an Adamite indifference to worldly things. And then once again the direct opposite, the total iconoclastic self-assertion of a Jimi Hendrix—of any columnist for *The Village Voice*; and now they have found the Greening of America through

Charles Reich's Consciousness III. But what Charles Reich says, if you boil it down, is what Robert Nisbet said quietly (and with style) when fifteen years ago he wrote about *The Quest for Community*. The kind of community Nisbet told us we all needed, and the kind that now Reich enjoins upon us, is inconceivable in the absence of individuation; and individuation is what happens when the state ceases to be taken for granted as the necessary instrument for human progress. The conservative who spoke to little audiences fifteen years ago about the necessity for arresting the growth of government was saying then what the followers of Reich have come upon, except that *they* are now condemning America, while what they ought to be condemning is what I once called the special effronteries of the twentieth century. One of these—Eastern seaboard liberalism—substituted ideology for metaphysics, causing that great void which the sensitive of whatever age feel so keenly. Those who are a little older, and expect less from an intractable world, come more readily to terms with their world, which is not to say that we accept it as it is, merely that we will not try to change it into something it cannot become, for no reason more complicated than that human hands are soiled.

I concluded that the continuing challenge of *National Review* is to argue the advantages to everyone of the rediscovery of America, the amiability of its people, the flexibility of its institutions, the great latitude that is still left to the individual, the delights of spontaneity and, above all, the need for superordinating the private vision over the public vision . . . Well now, *there* is a program for Mr. Nixon. Question. Reading this kind of stuff, how does it work into the practical consciousness of a Chief of

State? Obviously he does not call in his staff and redraft a forthcoming State of the Union Address. Will Mr. Nixon, even at the urging of his staff, actually read a deeply exploring essay by Burnham, or Hart, in search of fresh and useful coordinates? Is there a rhetorical fall-out? Or—*can* the President *read*? I do not mean here to distinguish between Nixon and other Presidents; I simply wonder. The super-worldly Ken Galbraith remarks in his diaries that when he went down to see the President-elect at Palm Beach, a few weeks before the inauguration, he gave Mr. Kennedy two or three books, intending not so much to instruct the President-elect as to divert him. Knowing Mr. Kennedy's appetite for eclectic reading matter, he gave him J. H. Plumb's *Sir Robert Walpole* and a volume of Betjeman's poems; and, to Galbraith's great surprise, he was informed by Jackie a day or so later that Mr. Kennedy had gone right through the books, late at night. Oh? How do they find the *time*? Where is the *evidence* that they have read it? Will the historians trained in a posteriori sleuthing say to us one day, "Kennedy obviously got this insight from the history of Walpole that Galbraith gave him to read." *Did* JFK read it? *Did* RMN read the *NR* essays? Galbraith has had much experience with students who have developed the art of pretending to have read books assigned to them; yet even with students one is careful, because it can be as painful to the monitor, as to the student, to uncover dissimulation. With Presidents, and Presidents-elect, one proceeds more cautiously, because it is not the business of friends, let alone subordinates, to quiz the President on his understanding of matter he has been given to read. That is why, for instance, one would not have said, "Mr.

President, what do you think of Burnham's thesis about the difference between the authoritarian and the authoritative state?" In the first place, one simply doesn't—not to a President, and not, after his sophomore year, to anybody else. In the second, a skillful politician could turn away the question easily; and the interrogator gets no probative satisfaction. Meanwhile the grillee makes a mental note to spare himself, in the future, the presence of this drillmaster.

We pass, on the New England Thruway just west of Bridgeport, the bloated oil tanks that bear the single marking BUCKLEY. For a thousand years, beginning when I was at Yale, I have been asked by those few friends and acquaintances who have passed by those hulks and have not *automatically* assumed that these are outposts of the Buckley fortune whether they are indeed my family's, and I have said No, they are not, tee hee, would that they were. The suspicious questioner at this point assumes that the fabled Buckley Fortune is too vast to be thus vulgarly advertised, on mere tanks. I mean, upperclass-folkways-wise, you don't go in for that kind of thing. If it happened that your great-grandfather was named, say, Hiram G. Coca-Cola, then there is no escaping the legacy. Otherwise, keep your name out of the commercial thing, particularly if you have a consumer product; much better. But when you endeavor to shake the conviction that the mastodonic oil deposits that guard growlingly the outskirts of Bridgeport reflect the size of your own financial resources, you receive the condescending smile that, soon now, I would receive from a student at the University of Bridgeport who would display amusement at my suggestion that it was neither factually nor symbolically correct that I was there to argue the case for the BUCKLEY oil interests in Bridgeport, *über alles*.

I arrive, as requested, at noon, and shake hands with a vaguely disconcerted committee which passes along the rumor that bad weather might delay the flight of Dick Gregory, who is bound from Cleveland to Hartford, whence he will be driven to Bridgeport. I am whisked off to meet Dr. James Halsey, the Chancellor, who is recovering from a heart-attack, and is permitted only today, after sixteen days' confinement, to receive a visitor—in the upstairs nursery at his home. He is proud of his Behemoth University (9,000 students, having at the close of World War II registered only a few hundred). I go off to lunch with fifty or so deans, sponsors, and alumni while reports file in, each of them gloomier than the last, concerning the movements of Dick Gregory; and then, before the dessert is served, the chairman tells me that it has been arranged for a helicopter to meet Gregory at the airport in Hartford, but that even so he could not be less than one hour late, leaving me with the burden of holding the attention of the crowd, which has come to witness a perfervid contest between a black revolutionary and an Ivy League conservative, and I experience the little ache that comes from knowing how infinitely disappointing it is to an audience to be deprived of the other member of a scheduled debate. (It has happened to me twice.) Would I undertake to deliver an address, about thirty minutes long, to be followed by questions from the floor until the arrival of Dick Gregory? The rule in such situations, which in variation often take place, is the ob-

96

vious one: you agree—to do what you can. I specify two conditions, the first that I be instantly relieved (we have not yet been served the dessert course), given an office where I might put together a thirty-minute talk (I know that that will involve simply shortening one of my current speeches, but that it will take concentration); and— condition the second—that in the event the helicopter brings Dick Gregory in ahead of schedule, i.e., before I am done with my thirty-minute talk, he be kept away from the gymnasium until I am finished. I know that if half or three-quarters of the way through an analytical talk, Gregory were to stride in, I could not hope to hold the attention of the audience; and to extemporize an emergency ending, like the organist who suddenly interrupts the fugue to launch into the wedding march because she sees that the procession has started, would be psychologically incapacitating.

Agreed. And a half hour later I am taken from the study in which I have been isolated; but the chairman discovers that he is fifteen minutes early. (It is very very bad to arrive fifteen minutes early at the hall where you are to speak, because you are at that moment nervous, even irritable, and there isn't anything that you can do or that can be done for you, to alleviate the tension; there isn't ever, anywhere, a little off-stage study where you can simply sit, and fuss with your notes, or turn on the television, or telephone your secretary.) So we drive through the park, and I am shown several civic attractions, told, even, the *ribald* legend given, by the kids, to an upright statue of a local inventor ("He discovered how you can do it standing up") and then to the gym, teeming with four thousand students and, outside, a long line waiting

97

for standing room tickets. I walk in and there is the usual ripple of appreciation, diminished by the news, already in circulation, that Gregory will be late (somehow, by the workings of the public psychology, I am vaguely to blame, perhaps only because I will profiteer from his absence by making my points unchallenged); and, in due course, with the promise that my antagonist would soon arrive, I am turned on.

I try a truncated version of the talk I gave the night before, wondering whether I might just discover, in this new version, that it is better communicated short than long. Gymnasiums are tough. The acoustics are always bad, and vocal inflections are difficult. The real pro, sizing up the situation, will adjust his voice accordingly; I *cannot* do so, which is why years ago I instructed my agent to warn my hosts about the absolute necessity of providing me with a sensitive acoustical system; and they try, they always do, but it seldom works so as to make communicable, to all the corners of the auditorium, soft-stated rhetoric. We move on to the question period, everybody wondering anxiously, I foremost among them, when, when, will Gregory arrive. Suddenly the presence is made felt, before even he steps into the hall, and now there he is a hundred yards away, exciting the audience as though Winston Churchill had walked in to answer a three-hour tirade by Clement Attlee.

"In sharp contrast," the Bridgeport *Telegram* wrote the next day, "and leaving no doubt where the students' sympathy lay, a long and loud ovation accompanied the delayed entrance of Mr. Gregory, who wore a blue wide-lapelled, double-breasted blazer, dove-gray bell-bottom pants, a thick beard and close-cropped hair." . . . The

98

applause deafening, he reaches the dais, and leans over gracefully to greet me—our first meeting in four years, when he had been my guest-adversary on *Firing Line*. "How are you, brother," he shakes my hand, vaulting over me in an uninterrupted motion, to occupy his seat, pending the hurried introduction of him; after which he bounds up to the microphone, holding it lovingly, professionally, to the indicated level . . .

"In perhaps intentional contrast to Mr. Buckley's urban sophistication and aristocratic tones, Mr. Gregory came on with easy, tough assurance, using earthy humor and the artless language of the streets. 'Black folks have put a lot of hope in the U.S. Constitution,' he said, 'but it never done'em any good. We never had a free society in America,' he maintained, 'and this was the one country where they laid foundations for a free society. Welfare? Don't tell me about welfare. The tax breaks for rich people: that's welfare in this country. I didn't start being on relief until I started making big money and paying for nothing. Rich people can write off their meals. Poor people can't,' he said. Almost every remark Mr. Gregory made was followed by cheers, shouts of 'Right On, Brother!' from groups of blacks, and applause." . . .

The theme of the debate was "Revolution or Evolution?," and concerning the depressing state of affairs in America Mr. Gregory was strictly non-partisan, indicting Republicans and Democrats alike . . .

"I hear a lot of people talking about revolution and repression these days [the (extraordinarily accurate) newspaper report went on]. They blame Nixon, Agnew, and Mitchell for the repression.

99

Well, you can blame those three for a lot of things, but repression is not one of them. If you want to find who to put the blame on for repression, it's *you*," he said, pointing a finger at the audience. "LBJ would have brought repression down on you, if you tried revolution; Kennedy would have brought repression down, too. You must understand that repression does more harm to the repressor than the repressed," he added. He compared the problems of this society to a teakettle that has begun to boil and whistle while the people in the room who had put it on the stove are too engrossed in a conversation to notice it. "Well so it goes 'Weeeeee!' and Mitchell, he's there in the corner, in the top bunk, and he don't like coffee anyhow, so he sends a couple of aides to plug the teakettle up," he went on, his features lighting up, the comedian now more to the fore than the activist. "And you don't hear no noise. For a couple of minutes," he pauses for a second. "That's repression," he concludes. . . . Using again another metaphor to illustrate the plight of American minorities, he said the civil rights problem is like a pregnancy. "American's pregnancy is just about over," he warned, "and when this baby is going to drop, it's going to drop, even if it means the death of the mother and the baby."

The program now requires the emptying of the gym (almost two hours have gone by), and the resumption of hostilities in a lounge in which only a few hundred students can fit, and thither we repair, to answer questions addressed alternately one for Gregory, one for Buckley.

100

At exactly four I finish an answer by announcing that, as I have informed the chairman of the ceremonies, I simply have to leave. "Shortly after Mr. Buckley left," the Bridgeport *Telegram* reported, "Mr. Gregory said of him, 'A lot of people think that Buckley is putting them on, but I believe that the cat is so honest, so ethical, that he do believe none of that bad bullshit exist, but it exists.' "

Had I been too easy on Gregory? I taxed myself the next day, sitting down to write a column about him. I recalled my debate at the Cambridge Union (England) with James Baldwin, in 1965: God, that was a rough one. A debate only in the technical sense, because Baldwin rose and was greeted with an ovation even *before* he opened his mouth to speak. I remember sitting there thinking, Boy, tonight is a *lost cause.* And, after his 25-minute speech was over, during which he was not once interrupted by a single student, notwithstanding that interruptions are the practice at the Cambridge Union, he sat down, while the crowd roared its approval. I rose, half-resigned, half-angry, because Baldwin, arguing the affirmative of the motion, *Resolved, That the American Dream is at the expense of the American Negro,* had—I thought, and think—made the flimsiest case to an audience unacquainted with his spectacular essay *The Fire Next Time,* so that I found myself telling the students that their treatment of Baldwin was the clearest testimony of their racial condescension, inasmuch as they could not reasonably have applauded his factual distortions except insofar as they desired to establish that they were instantly available to encourage any anti-American intellectual provided he was a Negro; and that, unlike

101

them, I was sufficiently lacking in racial prejudice to permit myself to become angry with a paranoid, notwithstanding that he was black-skinned. Oh dear. I lost the debate, by popular count, 3-1—or was it 30-1? I did not handle Gregory in that way, although what he said at Bridgeport—and says everywhere—is quite simply outrageous: and I found myself wondering whether I was slipping into that same condescension that I had accused the students of Cambridge of being animated by. Several days later I would receive two letters about the exchange, in exquisite contrast with each other; one of them taking off from the column I wrote. I said . . .

It is sad to see Dick Gregory, the comedian turned evangelist, signing (along with Ossie Davis) a money-raising letter in behalf of the Black Panthers, so I was glad of the opportunity (recently, at the University of Bridgeport), to discover what exactly are his views on the Panthers, and for that matter on things in general, several years having gone by since I first came across him.

My attitude toward him may be colored by his having on one occasion leaned over and whispered to me [it was after the *Firing Line* taping] that he had advised his wife and friends that I was a "beautiful cat." I have aspired to many things, but was never so ambitious as to dream that I would be called that by Dick Gregory. In turn I told him how moving I had found his book, an autobiography titled—unfortunately, I think—*Nigger*. And so we have proceeded to listen to one another: and what I hear is in one sense disheartening, in another sense not.

Mr. Gregory is a force in America. Particularly on the college campuses, where he comes on very strong, very strong indeed. He has spoken at 300 campuses during the last ten months, and is beginning now a tour of Canada, where he likes to begin by complimenting the audiences, which are so eager to think ill of America, on how well they treat their own Negroes. Big Applause. Then he says: "All 12 of them." [Gregory had told me this during the chairman's introduction, before we began the question period.] Gregory, as I say, is a professional comedian, with a comedian's sense of timing, and although he nowadays does only one or two night-club appearances per year he keeps in shape, he tells me, by waking up a good roll (as they say in vaudeville) for the first 15 minutes of his speeches. The jokes are highly political, tendentious, like the ones that made Mort Sahl famous. There are (generally speaking) three classes of enemies. The Southerner, the rich man, and the bureaucrat. It is Mr. Gregory's contention that America is run for the benefit of the rich man, an interesting point and, if so, a large chapter in the history of masochism, inasmuch as the very rich are taxed at the rate of 77 cents on the dollar.

On the matter of the Black Panthers Mr. Gregory was very serious. What he said was that the Black Panthers had come along, even as at different times in recent American history other groups had come

103

along, beginning with the NAACP, on through CORE, and then SNCC. That the Black Panthers give special solace to a large number of Negroes who, were it not for the Panthers, would engage in violence. He gave as an example an hysterical woman who, although a stranger, reached him by telephone insisting that a white policeman was seeking her out, intending to gun her down. Gregory gave her the number of Black Panther Hq., and the BP's sent over a bodyguard. He stayed with the woman, who after two or three days quieted down.

I ventured that such a treatment of the Panthers is the current version of the cliché of the twenties, that after all Mussolini had made the trains run on time: that what is remarkable about the Panthers isn't the machismo of their sense of concern for their people but the poisonous rhetoric with which they seek to infect the interracial dialogue: the racism which Mr. Gregory, in other contexts, deplores.

Undoubtedly there are Negroes who believe so strongly that America is racist that they deduce from that reality the necessity to hate the white race. Mr. Gregory informed the audience that two examples of our racism were 1) our incarceration of the Japanese population during the war, while leaving the Germans alone; and 2) our dropping of the atom bomb on the Japanese, while refraining from doing any such thing against the Germans. I pointed out that the California Japanese were removed because there was panic (unjustified) over the prospect of Japanese landings on the coast of California, and that after all the same man who superintended the operation, Earl Warren, twelve years later ordered the integration of the schools, and can hardly be thought of as a racist; and that we could hardly have used the atom bomb on Germany, inasmuch as we didn't have one until after the Germans were licked; and that anyway, we had killed five times as many Germans in raids on Dresden as we did Japanese at Hiroshima. Mr. Gregory smiled and, who knows, listened: and if he reads these words, I wish him to know that they come from a well-wisher who, to be sure, wishes he'd get his facts straight, and give the BP's a wide berth.

In reply to which, a tough answer from Marina, California. (Interestingly enough, the author of the letter typed in his telephone number. Interesting because the tone of the letter was not of the kind that encourages an instant-communication reply.) The letter suggests the special stiffness one runs into when pursuing trans-ideological understanding where on top of everything else, there is race to worry about.

Dear Mr. Buckley: Any nigger you would love, or who could call you "beautiful cat" and mean it, really is bound to be one.

It is "the worst form of niggerism to hook and jab, cut and stab at other blacks." (George Jackson telling what his parents taught him long before Black Panthers came on the block.)

Seeing blacks cut up each other must please you

105

mightily. [You wonder, what black did Gregory cut up? None. And you wonder further at the implications of such pressures as this, directed at proscribing *any* criticism by *any* black man of *any* other black man.] It keeps them apart, and the last thing a man like you could stand would be having black men all get together. Niggerism isn't restricted to the black community. For whites in a position to harm blacks, and who cannot resist doing so, practice niggerism. The difference is: when whites do it it is called racism, and the ones who do it are called pigs. But why do I bother to enlighten you?

For Christ's sake get away from blacks and let them alone to work out their own destiny. The best thing you can do, if you think you have a mission to help black people, is to direct your heavy artillery on the white community, where the racism is. To date the score is: you have amply demonstrated your ignorance of the Black Panther Party by calling them racists. I suggest you read Seale's book, "Seize the Time."

In one fashion or another, Buckley, you have to cure your own racism. It's up to you. Nobody can do it for you. Farthest from doing it would be hanging out with a black man who thinks you are a "beautiful cat." You could make a beginning with Charles Silberman's "Crisis in Black and White," John Hersey's "The Algiers Motel Incident," and "The Autobiography of Malcolm X." After you think you have cut your milk teeth, try Frantz Fanon's "The Wretched of the Earth," and George Jackson's "Soledad Brother." You won't believe your eyes,

106

ears, or sixth sense. You might even begin to *see* black people for a change. And you will find it a welcome change from your present course.

Good God, Buckley!

And the other letter, from a girl.

Since I'm a student at the University of Bridgeport I waited until after the debate [to write]. Anyway, since there wasn't any debate, which was a real disappointment, I was struck by the difference in tone between your speech and Mr. Gregory's. Not the surface things, sass-the-mastah vs. gallant courtliness, but Mr. Gregory's poorly concealed condescension and his perfectly beautiful tactical error. We college students are parvenu adults and, justly, sensitive about our ascribed status and questionable origins. Every time Mr. Gregory called us youngsters I snickered rudely—proving his point—and watched people deflate.

But you treated us far too well. You must remember that we are no better than we should be and certainly don't deserve a speech as rich as yours and with the mutual respect for intellect that it implied. I am not condemning myself and my peers for no reason at all. As Haim Ginott [a baby doctor] would say, I am very angry. Recently the chairman of our Political Science department gave a luncheon lecture on "Pop Maoism." Dr. Van der Kroef is a solid conservative and a rather difficult man to get along with. He was more or less retaliating for a series of lectures on Communist China, liberal slant. The

publicity people for the lectures made the unfortunate mistake of dubbing the series "China Week"
which made it sound like a promotional giveaway
for a bank, but they were very popular. Anyway,
several of my more liberal classmates were turned
away from the [anti-Communist] lecture. Cha-
grined, they stomped off and returned with a pig,
which they proceeded to roast in front of the student
center. As Dr. Van der Kroef left he was presented
with the pig's head. We Spock-spawn have limited
and primitive ideas of self-control but we are *terribly*
creative.

The point is, how do you deal with this kind of
witlessness? Perhaps Mr. Gregory does have our
number. Do you suppose liberalism is simply a stage
of development, something eventually outgrown, or
is it a pathological state that should be treated more
with pity than with scorn? I harp on this not only
because of the speech or the pig but something else
that happened recently.

I went to a lecture in New Haven given by Tim
Wohlforth of the Workers' League, supposedly a
more radical split with the American Communist
Party. Granted that this speech was directed to people who know the subject and are involved in the
Communist effort, people that were directly concerned with the Trotsky split and the problems of
revisionism: granted too that the question of Dia-
lectics is vital to the growth of the Communist
movement in this country. Correcting for all this,
Tim Wohlforth still comes across as ineffectively and
pedantically as my most ineffective and pedantic

English professor. Furthermore, as a conservative escorted by a young communist (I had picked him up on a street corner selling [Party] papers in the best Horatio Alger tradition), instead of being threatened or even ideologically roused by the lecture, I found myself not only totally unimpressed by the Red Menace, but, God help me, my maternal instincts raised by the kind of poor but honest idealism and the unquestionable reassurance that with communists such as these we need never tap another phone.

Their project for the next day was covering an auto plant, this was before the GM strike was resolved, and I knew then and know now that their objective of selling dialectical materialism to the auto workers in Framingham was doomed to failure by boredom, or, the All-American Huh?

What I am trying to say, I guess, is that I have despaired of selling anything at all intellectually. In fact, I find myself retreating to a kind of anti-intellectuality. The pig-roasters are a perfect example of over-education (as I am), but what do [you] suppose they would be doing if they weren't in college? I don't even want to think about it. And, if the Workers' League chokes and gags on a surfeit of theory and none of our pragmatism, I am, naturally, more than pleased. But I can't help wondering what would happen to conservatism if it were not for your considerable charisma. It's a stinken word of course, but I wonder after a while if it is this instead of concepts that sell an ideology. And then, from this I make a kind of bewildering jump to wonder if education is all that it promised to be in this country. I don't know if our wholesale educational process has done us any good at all.

Well, I wish I could say I was stoned the way all the other kids do when they write you, but, prices being what they are, it's only a Laredo.

Her doubts are of course shared by many who are discouraged by the failure of general education to achieve eudaemonia. Others, whose expectations were never high, are if not less discouraged, less disillusioned. Very early—I suppose because I had set out to read all his books (primarily because he was a close friend of my father's)—I read Albert Jay Nock's *Theory of Education in the United States,* the Page-Barbour lectures he delivered at the University of Virginia in the early thirties. Nock predicted even then that the effort towards universal higher education would most certainly not succeed; that the question was, Would it ruin true education for the few whom nature created educable? The verdict isn't in by any means, but the academic turbulence of the past few years suggests that the rationalists' certitude that more education would bring a higher level of discourse is chimerical. What we don't yet know—or at least what I don't yet know—is whether Nock's pessimistic prediction —that the truly educated few would begin to disappear —will prove to be the corollary reality. Those who cling to optimism should reflect that in 1850 there were ten times as many illiterates in America as in 1960, and during that period we traveled from the debates of Lincoln vs. Douglas, to those of Nixon vs. Kennedy. The anomalies are what always astound me.

110

I knew once, as a close friend, Professor Revilo Oliver, who was last heard from when the press noticed that he had written in some bizarre journal that the Pentagon, knowing ahead of time that John Kennedy would be assassinated, had secretly rehearsed his forthcoming funeral. Revilo Oliver being without any exception the single most erudite man I have ever known, I remember taking him aside ten or twelve years ago with considerable trepidation after getting a whiff of some of the rhetoric that was belching out of a right-wing committee he had joined. It was late at night, after all the speeches, at a bar, and I proffered my misgivings, insisting that in right-wing politics, too, distinctions must be made, and he replied with a twinkle, in his measured way, "Bill, before you got me interested in politics, I'd as soon have split the skull of anyone who split an infinitive, but in *politics* what matters is that you pull together." I was talking with a man whose scholarly exactitude eventually brought him around to buying eight custom-made typewriters, severally reserved for the work he does in the eight languages he commands, a precisionist who decided, at age 17, that he would never misplace a letter on the typewriter, and never has—or at least not in any of the hundreds of reviews and communications I ever saw. A few months after our conversation at the bar, he would be talking about the "thousands" of registered Communist agents who work in the Department of Health Education and Welfare.

During two summers we cruised together for a fortnight with Peter, and Pat, and two or three of the crew I used to race with, and I never knew better company than Revilo's. He is the size of Belloc, and his sense of humor and resources of wit are unmatched in my experience. But then in due course we had to drop him from the masthead of *National Review* after one spectacularly irresponsible speech, and when *National Review* went on to attack the John Birch Society, of which he was a director and its single literary light, there was silence, interrupted by a single visit. It was at his home, to which he had frequently invited me over the years. Now I redeemed the invitation, probably to his embarrassment. But he had only the alternative of explicitly rejecting me, because I was to speak at the University of Illinois, where he teaches and lives, and had to spend the night somewhere in Urbana. It was late, after the speech, and we were alone, but it was difficult sometimes to hear him because there were strange noises coming out of the kitchen, noises like a tape machine being run at fast speed with the volume left up; and indeed that was what it proved to be. I discovered that the scramble was the voice of General Edwin Walker. The general had recently been brought back from Europe for excessive and undifferentiated anti-Communism, and soon embarrassed the entire conservative community, which had presumptively backed him, when, interrogated by a Senate committee, he betrayed a Birchite ignorance of any distinctions, shored up by his indecipherably documented certainty that everyone in sight was an agent of the Communist Party. Well, General Walker was now running for governor of Texas, and the commotion in the kitchen was caused by the arrival at Revilo's of a tape of Walker's most recent speech, which the communicants of Urbana, Illinois, were coming in, one by one, to duplicate on their own tape recorders, like early Christians

112

come to copy the latest tablet from St. Paul. And of course the way to record fast, in order to facilitate the traffic, is at super-high speed which, when you play it to listen to, you then switch back to normal speed. In due course I asked Revilo how did he account for *National Review*'s turning against the John Birch Society, knowing what he did about the anti-Communist resolution of the editors of *National Review*. He replied that there were three possible explanations. The first, he said, was that I had been seduced into this insanity by the editors, whose judgment was tragically awry. The second, he said —a trace of apology in his voice—was that I reasoned that the ascendancy of Robert Welch jeopardized my own preeminence as a leader of the conservative movement, that I was motivated by reasons of personal vanity, and the appeal of power. Yes, I said; and the third? The third, said Revilo (Revilo speaks very slowly and precisely)—the third explanation, he said, "is that you are an agent of the Communist Party." I smiled, stretched out my legs, and asked: "Which of the three explanations do you lean to?" He replied, softly, but always precisely, "I lean toward the first two."

A year or so later Revilo got into real trouble. The trustees of the University of Illinois having heard about the article in which he explained the causes of Kennedy's assassination, entertained a motion to strip Revilo of tenure. I wrote a column hotly defending his rights and calling attention to his scholarly achievements, while dismissing his assassination treatise as moonshine, and found waiting for me a few days later, on returning from a trip, a small package with my name neatly lettered in Revilo's inimitable script, inside it a tiny facsimile of a Florentine knife, and on the card: "To stab your next friend in the back with, if you have another friend." . . . My question, Mr. Chairman, is: If it can happen to Revilo Oliver, are we surprised that it happened to Dick Gregory? He *do* believe that bullshit.

It's another question altogether why do the worldly of this community, as distinguished from the fanatics, countenance it? The Community moved against Revilo, all right, right-wing lunacy being unendearing; but the Community does not *impartially* deplore extremism. It appears that the intellectual and moral tension between two different worlds, the sane and the insane, isn't one our thought-leaders wish to eliminate by effecting an unconditional surrender of the infirm world. The co-existence of the two worlds, the Tedious Lunatic right, and the Interesting Tortured left, the intelligentsia are not so much reconciled to, as delighted by.

I was told a few years ago by a student at Princeton University of his having heard Estes Kefauver, who was campaigning in the New Jersey Presidential primary in 1956, deliver a speech to the graduate students. Kefauver was about an hour late, had delivered seven speeches during the day, and now he began his eighth, and after a moment or two the listeners, to a man, were seized by an agonized embarrassment; then, just as suddenly, as though the main switch were turned off, they relaxed. These young scholars all realized that the Senator was too dazed to focus on the nature of his audience, and was giving them the identical speech he had given during the day to the crowds in New Jersey, and you sensed their appreciation at knowing what are the necessarily demagogic habits of Real Life. Not at all, according to the

114

witness, any residual sense of frustration; of disillusion, of disgust, of hostility, engendered by the low quality of the analysis or of the emotions. "American society is dedicated to death," Professor Howard Zinn would say in debate with me at Tufts a few weeks after the meeting with Gregory: and there was not an intonation of protest from any one of the four thousand students there. And yet if the professor was using the words rigorously, as the context seemed to suggest—to condemn the Vietnam War as an expression of our society's sadism, or necrophilia—then he was saying something outrageously untrue and dishonorable. If he intended to mint a metaphorical use for the phrase "dedicated to death," its meaning was inscrutable, and the audience might *at least* have registered its confusion. Is the only response to the continuing phenomenon of selective indiscrimination, such a philosophical condescension as Albert Jay Nock developed into art? Perhaps. But such condescension is—well, Un-American.

We reach 37th Street, my brothers' offices; Jim is there, wrapping things up (or maybe he is dictating political matter, I don't think to ask), but my appointment is with Dean Reasoner, a partner in the family company, and its principal lawyer, whom I had asked to meet with Peter Starr and me, in anticipation of a board meeting of the Starr Broadcasting Company the next day.

Peter is the president and I am the chairman of the board. Peter was born on Pearl Harbor day, came to work for me at age 12 as cabin boy and crew on my sailboat, and worked for me every summer thereafter until, on graduating from Georgetown, he took a job as assistant salesman for the little radio station *National Review* had bought in Omaha, Nebraska, on which we managed to lose money, even though we had intended that it should make up the losses incurred by the magazine. Within five months, Peter persuaded me with a battery of letters analyzing the operation of the station to make him manager, the youngest, it transpired, in the country. A few months later he announced (at age 23) that he intended to buy a station in South Dakota, on his own, in the event that *National Review* did not want to buy it. The directors voted there and then, in the light of their unhappy experience with Omaha, to divest themselves of Omaha; and Peter and I together borrowed the money to buy it, and South Dakota. Two years later, our corporation went public, at which point we also owned stations in Kansas City, Houston, New Orleans, and Memphis.

Dean Reasoner happily combines legal rectitude with superhuman ingenuity, and we give him now what to others would be a circle-squaring problem—namely how to accomplish X, without diminishing the rights of Y. In his measured way, he nudges us in the right direction. He has the faculty, where legal problems are concerned, of releasing, say every fifteen minutes or so, a gossamer blanket over your impetuosities. You wrestle under it, finally poking your head through, at which point he lets drop the next one; and you repeat the process. Four or five layers later, you have reached the surface. The technique is to face the one complexity at a time, and he is skilled at withholding the incremental complexity, so that by the time it comes you are refreshed, and ready to crack it; an hour or two of this kind of thing and you are airborne, by contrast with the quicksand into which so many lawyers solemnly and exultantly plunge you when you approach them with your problems.

I can't leave Dean now, and need therefore to cancel an appointment at the Harvard Club with Henry Regnery, founder of Henry Regnery Co., publishers of *God and Man at Yale*, an old friend who comes to town only infrequently from Chicago. He is an enthusiastic conservative, a Germanophile who studied in Bonn before the war, and started his publishing company shortly after it, setting out to prove that a non-New York based publishing company can make it; but who has yet to prove it. Now he has passed along the principal executive responsibilities to his son-in-law, who is apolitical and (it is rumored) resists, as financially unproductive, the penchant of his father-in-law for conservative-oriented books. Henry is not a Catholic, although his family was, but his staple, during the fifties, was Catholic, or Catholic-oriented books: he rejoiced in producing books of scholastic philosophy, while attempting to run his publishing house on a budget most straitened, which resulted in the estrangement of many of his original modern-conservative authors. "If Henry Regnery alienates one more conservative author," Willi Schlamm said to me in 1955, with the pointed zest that made him beloved and hated in the Luce empire, "pretty soon he will have only Thomas Aquinas writing for him." I related the quip to Whittaker Chambers, a good friend of both Willi and Henry, who enjoyed it hugely, as I still do, regretting that Henry's house did not prosper, and reflecting that neither has any publishing house done so, in my time in America, merely by specializing in conservative-oriented

117

books. It wasn't until Neil McCaffrey thought to begin first a Conservative Book Club, and then to found a publishing house (which is, at least to a certain extent, a gathering system for the book club), that the operation became commercially viable. A year ago Neil called me in Switzerland to tell me that his publishing complex, owned at that moment by a faltering computer firm, was up for sale, and proposed that the Starr Broadcasting Company buy it. I called Peter, in due course the deal was made, and now the enterprise goes along nicely.

We have covered the subject, so Peter and I leave 37th Street, and move with palindromic assurance to 73rd Street, where we have dinner with Pat, in the lovely little red-orange library she created, where we hang the irresistible oil-and-crayon portrait of Carmen de Lavallade by her husband, Geoffrey Holder, her mulatto-made-primitive face cocked slightly, poignantly, eyes glancing down, a bouquet of flowers nestling in her hands; flanked on the right by Calliyannis's striking portrait of his 14-year-old son, in broad diagonal brush-strokes, Goya-colors; and, opposite, a peaceful, endearing Cerbellini, a dozen children watching a puppet show, inquisitively, shyly, suspensefully. In between, three by de Botton (my favorite): a guitar-player, his chord-hand in skeletal reds blues and oranges, as if his fingers had fused with the vibrant strings; an impression of Good Friday, with eerie browns and yellows; and an impression of the city of Toledo, seen at night, the orange shell small and central, a yellow, sullen moon, dark, mysterious browns—of all of my paintings, my favorite. We ate, and talked, the record played harpsichord music, the portable table is covered with lace and candles (Pat does not Compromise), and

118

Peter reverted to the joys and sorrows of the Starr Broadcasting Company. My family apart, I am as fond of Peter as of any human being. Indeed I feel for him that special affection I reserve for anyone who has made me a million dollars. He is still in his twenties, and I can experience the excitement he feels at having created what he has created, and I envy him the convenient standard by which he can judge his successes: the balance sheet, so miserably unavailable to the influence-merchants.

After dinner I make a determined move to my little study upstairs. I must spend a few hours reading over the material Aggie has got together for me, because tomorrow morning, at nine, I am to be at the Waldorf-Astoria in order to debate with Ramsey Clark before the annual convention of the National Association of Manufacturers; poor manufacturers, what a day: Clark and me in the morning, Goldwater at lunch, Nixon at dinner. At one A.M., I tread softly into the bedroom and turn off Pat's television set, and she mumbles reproachfully that she is carefully listening to the eleven o'clock news, which terminated one hour and thirty-five minutes ago, thank God, I wish the news was always over.

FRIDAY. At first it was ten o'clock, then nine o'clock, then would I be there for breakfast at eight? Frances told them I would be writing my column at eight, which is what I *should* have been doing at eight. Instead I was reading the New York *Times*, by which I am enslaved, and so I get there at nine exactly, only to find, as so often is the case, that I could have got there at nine-thirty just as well. It is the fashion, after one definitely and firmly

119

gives up lecturing—and only then—to write a valedictory essay of practical advice to lecture-hosts. It was done (hilariously) twenty years ago by Bernard DeVoto, and later by Dylan Thomas (also hilariously, except that he was not able to avoid, or else did not try to do so, the usual anti-American business). When I do mine, I shall suggest that a little room be set aside in which a host or a host's representative will padlock the speaker—to dispose of any anxiety about his whereabouts—and that ten seconds before he is required onstage, the room be unlocked. As it stands this morning, I am deposited in a public antechamber by a kind and attentive gentleman, and in due course Mr. Ramsey Clark is brought in, and I greet him. I had never met him—or even seen him on television—but last night I read reviews of his book, *Crime in America,* and one or two chapters from it. He is, currently, the principal human political enthusiasm of Dr. Robert Hutchins, who, it is reported, wants Clark to run for President, to be elected, and, one supposes, thereupon to enact Mr. Hutchins' new Constitution. Eric Sevareid comes in—he will be the moderator—and he is looking awful. He tells us he is suffering from the flu. Ushers, usherettes, and dignitaries flow back and forth, and eventually the hour strikes, and we are led out into the Grand Ballroom.

. . . The last time I was onstage there was three weeks ago, walking in behind Jim and his elated staff, the ballroom a madhouse which finally quieted down for long enough to hear his short victory statement. Then I *knew* he was dazed, because I heard my shy, modest brother uttering the words, "I am the voice of the new politics." I teased him later by sending him, framed, the headline in

120

the New York *Post* the day after the election, "BUCKLEY: 'I AM THE NEW POLITICS,' " getting back from him a winced note of pain at this lapidary record of what looked like a lapse into rodomontade. ("Who does Jimmy think he is?" I had scrawled over the headline, to my sister Priscilla. "La nouvelle politique, c'est goddam well moi!" Thus showing that Jim must *never* trade vainglories with me.) . . .

We sit down, and Eric Sevareid delivers introductory remarks, lengthy, wise, moderate, elegant—he is a very good writer—on the theme "Dissent Within a Lawful Society." He introduces Ramsey Clark, who begins his twenty-minute statement. One observes *very* intently an unknown speaker with whom one is debating, not unlike —I cannot resist the analogy—the matador observing the bull: his approach to the subject of course, his command of the subject, the character of his appeal to the audience, or to one part of the audience; and, very closely, one looks for his particular querencia, which is the Spanish word, so useful, for the area, quite arbitrary, that every bull chooses, towards which, when wounded, he returns, to make his last stand. Clark's is: the epistemological liberalism of John Stuart Mill, the notion that so long as any dissent exists, it is unsafe to assume that a society has got to the truth of a question. I have fought in that querencia often enough, and am familiar with defensive and offensive techniques. Clark is at once homespun and mellifluous; and every now and then just a little grandiose, e.g., "Dissent has been the principal catalyst in the alchemy of truth," which sentence, substituting as it does "in the alchemy of" for the simpler "of," suffers not only from straitened grandiloquence, but from an edgy syntactical ineptitude, because if he was determined to use "in the alchemy of," he should have said "in the alchemy of truth-seeking," right?

On the homespun front he asks, "Why was Roger Bacon called the 'father of science'? We remember the story. [That is good oratorical practice, flattering the ignorant, and admitting the learned into one's company.] Bacon was in the monastery; they were writing a new encyclopaedia. The question was the number of teeth in a horse's mouth; a bitter debate went on for several days, and there were three theories—thirty-two, thirty-four, and thirty-seven. Everybody had firm documentation for his position. Some went back to St. Augustine, some to various papal encyclicals. Roger Bacon, not a particularly energetic person and somewhat of a dreamer, was looking out the window and he saw a horse, and had the temerity to suggest that they go count the number of teeth in the horse's mouth—and that, of course, is the day that he was excommunicated from the church, and that is why he is called the 'father of science,' because he would seek the truth."

I did not recall that Bacon had ever been in a monastery, doubted strongly that he was ever a Catholic, was under the impression that no encyclopaedia was ventured until the century after his death, and knew very well that he was the greatest establishmentarian toady of his time: but wasn't sure enough of myself, so I didn't note down to challenge Clark on the point; and anyway, he who lives off the exposure of sciolism will die from the exposure of sciolism. (I was never in my life luckier for having indulged my prudent instincts. I engaged family and friends with the hilarious biographical solecism of

122

Ramsey Clark while writing these notes; and then—and I simply cannot account for the cause—suddenly, at about four o'clock one morning, I woke up, and the only reason I did so was that Mother Providence was knocking insistently on my door. And the message was: He said *Roger* Bacon, ass, not *Francis* Bacon. Great God! How close I came!)

Clark's general approach harmonizes with the Greening Impulse of Charles Reich ("Do you really understand how taxi drivers feel?"). And again, the formal democratic epistemology of J. S. Mill: "If the idea is wrong, is there any better way to demonstrate it than to really expose it? Is there any better way to make it more dangerous than to repress it?" And the people-to-people peroration. "If we give people the opportunity to speak, then their emotions cannot overflow. If we listen, if we try to learn, if we point out the error of their ways, if there is such error, if we aren't afraid to hear another point of view—and, if we are, we will never meet the challenge of today and tomorrow. To me, the First Amendment is more than a thing that talks about free speech, saying you've got to tolerate the point of view of others; it speaks of the spirit of humanity, the right to think, to be let alone, to breathe, to speak and assemble and to pray. And, if we don't insist on that for all of our people, we won't have it for any. And, in the vastness of the changes with which we are confronted, we should never forget the words of John Kennedy: 'Those who make peaceful revolution impossible make violent revolution inevitable.' Thank you." Applause.

As he sits down, I decide to begin by poking a little fun, drawing on the public feud between Clark and J. Edgar Hoover, ventilated last week in connection with the publication of Clark's book. What the hell, why not? "Thank you, ladies and gentlemen; thank you, Mr. 'Jellyfish' Clark, as he is called down in Washington . . ." Most of the crowd recalls that last week Hoover said of Clark that as Attorney General he had been a "jellyfish." They are mildly amused, though a little nervous at this sudden rending of the petit-point sweetness. Important to pay Clark, therefore—and right away—his due, lest I needlessly estrange the audience, which I often do. "I do think that the most engaging thing about Mr. Clark is his transparent sincerity; the most difficult thing about Mr. Clark is his utter confusion. It is a rather beguiling confusion, because it issues not out of bad but out of very pure motives. He desires an improvement in the lot of man, and we must assume that the discussion today will not tend to divide those who desire such an improvement and those who desire to impede it." And, with a few preliminaries, on into the point. "In his book Mr. Clark seems always to be saying that that which would happen, were we to open up our ears and permit it to happen, would bring us into a kind of paradise the only alternative to which is the violent revolution with which, in his peroration, Mr. Clark threatened us. There are a lot of things wrong with that analysis. For one thing (and I don't think this is any clearer to Mr. Clark than it was to Oliver Wendell Holmes), what are the consequences of his own epistemology? He says that the principal catalyst —that dissent is the principal catalyst in the alchemy of truth. But I think he would find it very embarrassing if asked to define what 'truth' is, or what are the consequences of happening upon it. Surely, if alchemy is an appropriate metaphor to use when you talk about truth, it means that, after you have experienced this dissent, after you have worked your way towards the discovery of truth, you've [finally] got hold of something. What is the point of discovering truth unless you face the logical consequences of branding its opposite as 'error'? And if, in fact, you are permitted to acknowledge that something is 'error,' what do you do about the voices that proclaim error? What is the purpose of seeking truth, if not acting on it? It would be preposterous for America to suggest we have discovered all truths. But it would be ungrateful to suggest we have not discovered some of them. People have died for those truths that we have happened upon in the American experience, and [others] are prepared to die for them once again."

I go on to say that unless dissent is defined so as to exclude, for instance, the prescriptions of such as William Kunstler, dissent will itself be dishonored, and in the ensuing public confusion, tyranny will threaten. I offer an example of the current confusion. "I was asked, recently at Rochester University, what concrete steps I might propose to help the judicial system [along], and I said, 'Disbar Kunstler.' Mr. Kunstler, who shared the platform with me, was displeased. And I was, of course, roundly booed, and my response was, 'Don't—don't boo *me*. Boo the rules of the Association of the Bar of the City of New York which admitted Mr. Kunstler to the practice of the law. Either disband those canons, or apply them.' And then I read just two or three sentences from Mr. Kunstler's interview in *Playboy* magazine, published the day before. He said, 'It is the role of the American left to resist rather than merely protest: to resist illegitimate authority.' 'So,' said the [*Playboy*] questioner, 'how do you define illegitimate authority?' He [Kunstler] named the authority that ordains the draft, the payment of taxes to support the war in Vietnam, 'the domestic and foreign policies of a government that crushes people on every level'—all the things in this society that 'tend to degrade and destroy people.' Mr. Kunstler was then asked how, specifically, one should go about breaking the law. Well, take the college situation. The students can take over their college by occupying its buildings, counseled counselor Kunstler. Just plain occupying them? No. The students should occupy the buildings pending the administration's capitulation. If the administration refuses to grant the student demands, they move one step further. 'Another form resistance could take would be the burning down of a particular college building. [To be sure, after evacuating it.] 'You condone arson?' Kunstler was asked. 'Yes,' said Kunstler. 'If a point has been reached in a given situation where the mechanisms of society are not responding to serious grievances,' then arson is an appropriate response.

"Speaking for myself [I go on, leaving Kunstler], I can count sixty-eight times during the period since my twenty-fifth birthday when, applying the Kunstler code, I would have felt compelled, personally, to put a torch to the White House. And, of course, Mr. Sevareid is quite right when he says that the Vietnam war is hardly responsible for it all. Mr. Kunstler says, 'I would hate to think the war in Vietnam could be the only catalyst for resistance . . . there is so much more that remains to be resisted: the oppression of black people . . . poverty, the unequal distribution of wealth,' and so forth. And yet, the Bar of the

City of New York [which proscribes the urging of extra-legal activity by its members] does nothing . . . And such indecisions reach down through the vibrations of public life and affect the whole structure of authority and the whole gravity of the legal and philosophical codes that are the understructure of the society. We are losing even the force of public sanction."

Mr. Clark, in his rejoinder, says, "Well, there is some advantage in speaking second, isn't there? I have no *real* rebuttal, really. I feel this way—that, if I am transparent, I want to be transparent. It's very hard to see the truth. I enjoy the banter of engaging in personalities, but I really think this country has issues. If we are to solve them, we have to address ourselves to them. We can. But, if we only engage in personalities we won't. [Polemically skillful. A form of paralepsis. "If *we . . . only . . .* engage in personalities": very effective.] I think we are going to have to look at dissent for what it is, and try to understand it." Applause

A few questions from the floor, and it is over. Well, not quite. A middle-aged lady is introduced by the master of ceremonies. She desires to ask the audience to consider, very briefly, her plan. She has been given five minutes to explain it, and she does, very sweetly, if just a bit coquettishly. It is this: why not everybody in the United States pause for one minute per day—the same minute, everywhere—to consider the problems of America, and the imperatives of love and compassion and charity? She wants us to try it ourselves, Right Now. And after we do so, to please fill out the questionnaire, which the ushers are already distributing, so that we can let her and her committee know what we think of the idea? Ready? SI-

127

LENCE. (I devote *my* minute to hoping that Harry Elmlark will be loving, charitable, and compassionate when he sees me walk in, a few minutes from now, *without* my column.) The minute is up, we rise, I ask the lady if it is all right if I complete my questionnaire back at the office, and she smiles, extra-sweetly, after her minute's nourishment. I shake hands with Mr. Clark, tell Eric to go to bed till he gets over his flu, and walk purposefully out; long steps, and always take the staircase when you can, lest you be detained. Important.

I leave the Waldorf and walk three blocks to the offices of the Washington Star Syndicate, in the Newsweek Building. I go there to write my column maybe six or seven times a year, when I a) am in New York, and b) recognize that I cannot postpone by even three minutes more the writing of my column. (The contract says something vague about delivering it in the morning. Actually, I can have it in as late as two in the afternoon, and there is still time to stencil, address, stuff it into the envelopes, and get to the post office by late afternoon; but today I have a one-fifteen lunch date.) I go there, too, because c) there is the further attraction of Harry Elmlark in his lair.

Harry is the nervous, extrovert president of the syndicate, who graduated from the University of Virginia many years ago and went during the depression years into the syndicate business, working for the late George Matthew Adams. It was a small operation, a few comic strips, household-aid columns, and—Harry's most remunerative achievement—Father, then Monsignor, then Bishop, Fulton J. Sheen. Adams died in the early sixties. Lacking the capital to buy the syndicate himself, Harry approached the Washington *Star*, and sold it (and himself) to them. He grew up an avid New Dealer who rejected an invitation to join the Communist Party (whose representative apparently thought him nubile for the proposition), who tolerated Eisenhower, hated Nixon, loathed McCarthy, distrusted MacArthur.

One day in 1962 as I was preparing to leave for Switzerland, Gertrude Vogt, who seldom spoke sternly to me during the fifteen years she was my secretary, told me that if I did not take this call from a Mr. Elmlark, of the George Matthew Adams Syndicate, she had to assume, from his persistence, that he would be waiting to meet me at the Geneva airport, so I picked up the receiver. It was a most extraordinary performance. Salesmanship is nowadays derogated, the assumption being that A Salesman is somebody who persuades you to do something you do not want to do. What H. Elmlark wanted me to do was flat-plain, he wanted me to write a once-a-week newspaper column. What Buckley did not want to do was to write a newspaper column—except under circumstances that he did not believe any syndicate would agree to, namely, a guarantee of a reasonable sum of money per column, and a contract of at least two years' duration. The terms were fresh in my mind when Harry called, because a representative of the North American Newspaper Alliance (NANA) had got from me a few weeks earlier, for year-end syndication, 1,500 words on the meaning of the American right wing, to run opposite 1,500 words from Gore Vidal on the same subject, for which 1,500 words we had been paid $150 apiece, as I remember. NANA had come back to me asking whether I would agree to do a weekly column, the proceeds of which they would share

129

with me 50-50. They were quite certain that in no time at all I would arrive at $150 per week. I declined: Not unless you guarantee me the $150 per week, I said. And there the matter stood, I reported to Harry Elmlark. I remember somebody telling me that the trick in selling is never to stop talking. If that is the trick, Harry is the master of it, because without drawing a breath he told me that he would guarantee me $200 per week, beginning April 1—a couple of months away—which would give him time to start selling the column. I knew nothing about him, or about George Matthew Adams, and did not even have time to wonder whether Fulton Sheen was too other-worldly to know if he was associated with a competent syndicate. But I was greatly taken by the enthusiastic babble at the other end of the telephone, and so I said, that being my way, Okay. I could hear the smile, as he wished me a safe trip, and told me that the contract would be along shortly after my arrival in Switzerland.

And indeed it was, and I read it with that glaze that comes over my eyes whenever I read contracts. The idea was that I would receive the first $200, the syndicate would receive the next $200, and after that we would split 50-50. I will never forget the excitement that H. Elmlark generated over the next six weeks, during which I received a letter from him every two or three days, each one of them relating a conquest, and the price that said conquest had agreed to pay for my column beginning April 1. Harry asked me, in his first letter, to please send him off, fast, two or three sample columns. I categorically refused, most conveniently citing reasons of principle: Why, I asked, should I have to write more, having written so much?—I could send him bushels of books, articles, editorials. More important I declined because I was then 37 years old, had seen published everything I wrote since at age 21 I became editor of the *Yale Daily News*, and had at that point contracted the conventional block of not being able to write except on the certainty that what I write will be published. Once again, Harry acquiesced, and I learned later that he did not send my old stuff to the editors, preferring to egg them on over the telephone, or in personal interviews, his sales pitch being that the Right Wing had become extremely important in American politics. (He was at least tactically prophetic: that fall, President Kennedy would denounce "right-wing extremists," a *Newsweek* cover was devoted to "Thunder on the Right." The Young Americans for Freedom would soon sponsor a gigantic rally for Senator Goldwater at Madison Square Garden.) By the end of March, Harry told me: we were off. He had sold a weekly gross of $340, leaving his syndicate comfortably in the profit margin, though short of its 50 per cent share. Much much later he confessed to me that the contract I signed in fact did not commit the syndicate to launching me, that he would *not* have launched me if he had met with a stone wall from the editors.

I remember the trepidation as I sat down, three days before leaving Switzerland, to write The First Column. I devoted it to an examination of an interview Malcolm Muggeridge had recently conducted with C. P. Snow, reprinted in *Encounter*, in which Snow had said, in answer to the question, "Where would you prefer to live, in the Soviet Union or in the United States?" that he, Snow, would find life in the two countries equally attractive. Or was it equally unattractive? Telephone call. Transatlantic, which isn't Harry's way. He thought the column a disaster (he used a euphemism), I must write a more timely one, etc., etc. So I wrote something about a quarrel between liberal and conservative Catholics, and though I could tell from the tone of his voice (*I* telephoned *him*) that he thought it less than what he had hoped for, it went off to the newspapers, and the column was launched. A few weeks later I contrived to use the Snow column, by the simple device (I was lecturing in California) of instructing Gertrude to advise Mr. Elmlark that unfortunately I had not been able to meet my deadline, and that therefore the only solution I could think of was to send out the Snow column. He took it in good grace (he always does).

Still I had not met Harry—I was back in New York for only a few hectic days before beginning a long lecture tour. And then, finally, he came to my office one day for a sandwich lunch, and, lean, fifty-fivish, dressed like the leading man in *The Boy Friend*, buoyant, springy in gait and conversation, we became, instantly and inseparably, friends. He told me that the principal criticism of my columns was that they tended to deal with more than a single subject, bad; that otherwise they were okay. By this time Harry had 30-odd clients, which he raised to 75 quickly, and then the figure leveled out. In the fall of 1964 he proposed that I write three times a week, and that his syndicate join with the mastodon King Features, 25-25-50 (50 for the author), in order to be able to merchandise the column in the little cities and towns his own syndicate could not hope to reach except over a much longer period. That was a considerable proposal which

132

would tie up a lot of my time and energy, and for once I hesitated, even after talking with my old friend Bill Mc-Learn, the serene, courtly president of King Features, who was anxious to make the deal. Bill assured me that within a year the column might be expected to bring in a thousand dollars a week, to which argument he added that in the coin of influence, the thrice-weekly columnist has ten times the clout of the once-a-week columnist. He gave the reasons why, which are plausible enough. They are based on the assumption that the unguided reader responds to the cumulative effect of a commentator's analyses; so that if you are not around, except once a week, he loses running touch with you. Since it is impossible to extrude the whole of your *Weltanschauung* in every column, the necessity is to inch it a little bit along, every couple of days, so that when you move in, say, on the Common Market, or the Vietnam War, the reticulations are still in focus, and the reader sits down with a comfortable sense of familiarity with what went before. And so on. And not unconvincing. The commitment seemed enormous, though, and I consulted with James Burnham. Jim had recently read the biography of Renoir by his son, in which he spoke of what JB called the "cork-theory" of human impulses, whether artistic or journalistic, the idea being that it sometimes pays to conceive of oneself as a cork, in contrast say to a mooring, the better to flow, as Renoir's style did, with the currents that tease it along. Bad philosophy; but not-so-bad, Burnham pointed out, as a guide in personal, professional matters —to move along like the cork makes presumptive good sense, if you want to stay grooved in with the vibrations of modern life.

So, beginning the first of the year, 1964, I sat still for the supplementary harness, and by now I have written well over a thousand of the things, and Harry is always there, commenting on what I write, indispensable not merely to one's vanity, but to one's sense of *motion*. A year or two later, in one of the great syndicate raids in modern journalism, Harry won over a columnist who, after only a year on the market, was flourishing with his own syndicate. Though the material inducements Harry offered were significant, the operative reason for the columnist's decision to go over to Harry was that he had not in the course of an entire year heard a single word from his syndicate manager, neither of praise nor of blame, and (the letters that come in from the readers are no substitute) the writer was going mad with loneliness; which doesn't happen to friends of Harry.

I say hello to the small staff, the editor, the secretary, the typist, the mailboy. Harry takes me into his office, tells me I am the highest-paid typist in the world, asks me what I intend to write about, gives me Frances's phone messages, produces a cup of coffee, describes triumphantly his morning's renegotiation with the Indianapolis *Star*, and moves noisily out of his office, even though I repeat my usual offer to write elsewhere. I make the phone calls, look at my watch, calculate that I must write without interruption, and resolve to write about Dick Gregory. Harry comes in after ten minutes, and takes page one for the typist, and in a half hour it is over, there being no extra research that needs doing (when I go to Harry's to write, I must write about something that has already been researched). Harry tells me an anecdote or two as I put on my overcoat, asks what are the pros-

134

pects for the Starr Broadcasting Company in which he has invested, walks out with me to the elevator. We go down, stopping, it always seems, at a dozen *Newsweek* floors, the ladies and gentlemen of the staff, bound to and from their lunch, shuffling in and out. There is conversation, which I discourage, never having acquired the habit of treating an elevator like a City Room, where anybody is free to talk resonantly, never mind that others can overhear. But Harry is oblivious of the other passengers and is perfectly capable of revealing a corporate intimacy in matter-of-fact tones, at conversational level, even as the elevator stops to allow in the 18th rider, and we crush together nose-to-nose. Looking down, I grunt my astringent responses as Harry goes on, while the elevator, SRO, listens silently, intently; and then the doors open, Harry finishes his story as we walk to the revolving door, we say goodbye, I spot my car, a few yards away, and step into it, making a pass at Rowley, who is sleeping in the front seat, and give Jerry the address of the restaurant where Sherry Lord is.

The restaurant is called Maxwell's Plum, somebody had told me I *must* try it, it lay midway between Sherry and me, so here we are; Sherry as shy and endearing as when I met him freshman year at Yale, a suite-mate during sophomore year, whom I had lost touch with, and now he is hard at work painting, earning his keep at the Brooklyn Museum, separated from his second wife. We pass a pleasant hour and a half, during which I tell him the truth, that I could not imagine, assuming one were good at it, a more pleasurable way than painting to make one's living, the difference from music being the obvious one—that there is a creation left over, after one's labors,

135

which hangs around, maybe for centuries. There is no time to go to his studio, but we fix a date a couple of weeks later, and I drive off to 73rd Street where, in one hour, the directors of the Starr Broadcasting group will assemble. Meanwhile, the mail.

A haunting letter from Maryland. One of those I do not feel like answering right away, preferring to think about it, so for the nonce, I merely acknowledge receiving it. It is from a young man named Herbert, a young teacher who also does graduate work . . .

I first heard from him several months ago. In that letter he had recounted a quite extraordinary experience. He had, I gather, expressed doubt to one or two of his radical friends about the seriousness of the revolutionary movement in which they were engaged. A few days later one of his friends approached him. If he would consent to the terms as thereupon specified, Herbert would be vouchsafed concrete evidence of the seriousness of the endeavor he doubted. He agreed, submitted to a blindfold and was driven by automobile for an hour or two, in what direction he could not guess. The car stopped, and he was led out into a grotto, or a barn—I forget—and there he saw the most formidable accumulation of weapons he had ever seen: rifles, pistols, grenades, explosives, mortars, the lot of them tucked away against the day when the Movement would decisively assert itself. I remember concluding from the tone of the letter that I was not being tousled by a Minuteman, or teased by a Weatherman: and so I wrote to a friend well-lodged in the hierarchy of the Federal Bureau of Investigation—for the second time in my life, when the purpose of my letter was a purely formal civic duty, the other time being when I

136

relayed an anonymous warning that if Senator Ted Kennedy participated in the anti-Vietnam agitations of November 15, 1969, he would be assassinated. I did not tell Herbert what I had done, but a few weeks later he was visited by the FBI and questioned, to what avail I do not know, knowing only that it happened: not because the FBI told me but because Herbert wrote and told me, indignantly. Not altogether indignantly, in fact, because his mind is of the orderly kind that recognizes the probable consequences of so provocative a communication addressed, if not exactly to a member of the Establishment, at any rate to someone whose relations with the Establishment are formally correct.

But he did demand as a minimal expiation for the broken confidence that I agree to lunch with him, inasmuch as he desired to elucidate matters he had raised in his letter. Okay, I said, and a date was set in New York, which I was required at the last minute to break. Frances told me that Herbert had expressed considerable dismay when she gave him the news, because a) he had bought a brand-new suit to wear at our lunch, and b) he had rather looked forward to visiting New York, which he had never laid eyes on, notwithstanding that he was born and brought up in Maryland, where he teaches, near Baltimore. So Frances proposed that he lunch with me in Baltimore on my way up from Chapel Hill, before my talk at the University of Maryland the following Thursday.

It was arranged, and he arrived at my hotel suite with a talkative, highly informed Catholic, also a teacher. We spent two hours together, Herbert in his mid-twenties, large, crew-cutted, homely, acutely intelligent, listening, for the most part, to his friend's diligent interrogations.

After Herbert and his friend left, I prepared for the speech concerning which he now has written me. A hectic prelude. A column to write. Then down to meet Garry Wills, who had come to fetch me in the lobby. He drove me to his home, where we listened to his super hi-fi, and then ate early. Garry, whose book *Nixon Agonistes* has shaken his old conservative friends, said grace before we attacked the fondue Bourguignonne, and he and Natalie and I, the children segregated to the corner of the kitchen, drowned out their talk and laughter with our own, which springs from ancient and trans-ideological affections. The head of the lecture series, a young man of enormous self-possession, arrived, dismayingly punctual but apprehensive about the hour, with two companions, to drive me faster than I have ever driven, to College Park, to a teeming auditorium, hot and tense, on the same campus that had conducted earlier this year an ugly strike during the Cambodian business. The overflow was packed into an adjacent lounge, there was a no-nonsense feel to the whole thing. After five minutes I had to take off my jacket and even then I had to rub my eyes every minute or so to blot up the sweat that made the text swim before my eyes . . .

Along with Herbert's letter about the speech, another letter, from a young historian, who gives his impressions of the event, gently reinforcing my own opinion of my shortcomings as a public speaker.

Arriving from Washington only half an hour before you were scheduled to appear, I found the hall outside the auditorium crammed with an overflow

138

crowd. The interesting thing about them was not so much their number as their diversity. Few of them were cast in the mold of YAF [Young Americans for Freedom], but your name and personality had attracted hundreds of them, ideologically uncommitted or left-leaning, and there was a genuine air of expectation. They stood patiently in line and then, when it became obvious that there was no more room in the auditorium, filled the corridors of the Student Center to listen to you over the public address system.

And they were really listening. I say this because I ended up in the midst of the great unwashed, and made a point of observing their reactions. It was the first time I have seen that many college students pay rapt attention to the unaccompanied spoken word in quite some time. What struck me about it was their obvious thirst for a coherent set of ideas and, even more important to them, ideals. Their own much-vaunted liberal "life-style" is devoid of both, and this is something they seemed to realize by their presence.

Probably wisely, you kept the tone of your remarks rather low-key. No ostentatious exhorting of the faithful or calling to the colors. Yet I was left with the suspicion that a little more prodding might have turned an interesting evening into a real turning point for quite a few of them. [The old complaint: the failure of the exegete who does not deign —perhaps because he cannot?—to lead.]

As it was, they were very impressed with William Buckley but he was still the exception to the rule for them—an exotic, interesting visitor from another world. You drew them in, captured their attention, and planted a few misgivings about government collectivism coupled with individual license. [I had delivered what I have here designated as my Number 2 speech.] But, for most of them, the whole thing will be put back into its "proper" perspective by faculty, friends, media and intellectual pace-setters in the months ahead. Perhaps this is inevitable, but it does seem a damn shame, and one could wish that after you had made initial contact there were some kind of systematic follow-through beyond the sincere but necessarily limited efforts of local YAF chapters. Whether there is anything more you could have done I do not know. As conservatives I suppose we share a distaste for appeals based on emotionalism. But I am more and more convinced that underlying any deep commitment to conservatism, there is an element of passionate belief (I happen to associate it with certain spiritual values too—hence my revulsion for the Ayn Rand brigade). Can this *feeling* for basic values be articulated before a large, mixed group? I am uncertain, but it has been this sort of shared emotional commitment, admittedly wan at times, that has kept Western civilization going, but seems to be guttering at the moment.

My misgivings were reinforced by a conversation I had with a local YAFer whom I knew from membership in a military history group a few years back. He is now a sophomore at Maryland and, being a student, and about six years my junior, could paint a clearer picture of student life today. The dimensions

140

of the drug situation (he told me that everyone in his dorm was able to buy any type of hard or soft drug they wanted, and usually did) seem to be cancerous. Since most of the people in this dorm were engineering and business majors, it is not just a problem with the flakier elements in the philosophy and literature departments. Both authorities and parents are either ignorant of the mess or unwilling to recognize its existence. All very somber.

Still, it was a most interesting evening, and after returning home and putting Handel's *Messiah* on, while adding the finishing touches to a Revolutionary War piece for *History Today*, some of the uneasiness dispersed.

I acknowledge the letter, and go down: Peter Starr and the directors are here.

We have business to transact, a lot of legal this-and-that to pass over, and one or two questions to discuss concerning prospective remuneration for directors, several of whom travel great distances for the board meetings and do the homework hard. They attend because they were, somewhere along the line, caught by the ray of Peter's excitement, and they throb with the energy of the management, and want to be in on it. We are acquiring a television station in Tennessee, five million dollars, an intricate financing in a seasick market, the banks and insurance companies and the personal underwriters at last lined up, as also the SEC, the FCC, Peat, Marwick, Mitchell & Co. and, it would not surprise me to hear, the New York *Times*. It is a long meeting, and finally, at

141

seven, I offer them drinks, and they prepare to fan back across the country. At seven-thirty I go up to dress. Because Pat and I will have dinner with Rosalyn Tureck.

I hadn't seen Rosalyn, to talk to, since the *Firing Line* broadcast. She had invited me (always by hand, always delivered by messenger to 73rd) to dine with her after each one of her three concerts, but I had declined, because I had guests at all three whom I wouldn't have ditched, and because I was uncomfortable at the prospect of dining with a super-star after a strenuous performance: What can you talk about? In Rosalyn's case, safely, about the magnificence of her performance. But after that, one drifts into other subjects, while feeling, somehow, that the great artist who has to listen to talk other than about her performance, while the applause still rings in the ear, is somehow let down. She gave a fourth date, and because it was she, and because we could not say No a fourth time, Pat and I resolved to break our rule, usually sacrosanct, that Friday nights we spend in the country.

She is there, at the Laurent, with three friends—an English painter, and her New York lawyer and his wife—and the evening proceeds rapturously. We talk about everything (except politics), dine wonderfully, everyone enjoying everyone, and Rosalyn tells me that the note I sent her, likening Bach's E-minor Partita to King Lear was right on, that she had played the partita a thousand times, but always treated it with awe because she could not know what it would say to her this time around, even as Lear cannot be tuned by stroboscope. I mention that a professor of music history at Yale, raw-boned, tall as

142

Kenneth Galbraith, shy but culturally cock-sure, had whispered to me once that that partita was It, and that I had come to its mystery and majesty quickly, ardently, had heard it played a hundred times, but never better done than by her at the first of her series, which as a matter of fact was the truth, and she is glad, particularly because the *Times* had given perfunctory notice to her series. We glow together, and she asks her guests would we care for a liqueur, and I suggest we should have one at 73rd Street, wink noisily at Rosalyn, and suggest that WHO KNOWS, the liqueur might just conceivably give her a hard case of cacoëthes piano-itis, she giggles her aristocratic warm giggle, leans over and whispers that she will play me the saraband she knows I love, and I have to avoid Pat's horrified stare, because Pat thinks that to ask an artist casually to play for you is like asking Picasso to please come on home and do your portrait, and she thereupon turns the situation uproarious, as is her special skill, into a scenario wherein Rosalyn's lawyer is there and then to draw me up a bill, but Rosalyn and I just coo, and walk into the car. We get home, and I fetch the liqueurs, snapping shut conversational spontaneities, lest Rosalyn should lose her resolution, and nudge her quietly but decisively towards the piano. At which point, just as she sits down and pulls out that talismanic handkerchief, the fondling of which precedes the contact of her numinous fingers with the keyboard, Horrible Foo gets into the act by, I gather, sinking his fangs deep into the forearm of the painter, causing Pat to make all kinds of motions simultaneously, rushing to get blood plasma or whatever, remonstrating with Foo, persuading the lawyer that it is really unprofitable to sue dog-owners, fetching extra brandy for the dazed painter; during all of which, or so Pat claims (oh, she would make a good story out of it), I am attempting to exact total silence from the room, so that Rosalyn might proceed; and in due course, Foo having been exiled, the tourniquet applied, the glasses filled, the excitement damped down, Rosalyn plays, and my cup runs over. I hope that on ending the saraband, she will decide that she wants to play more and more and more. But she rises, whether because she does not *want* to play more, or because she resists instinctively the an-evening-with-Gershwin-is-a-Gershwin-evening temptation, I do not know. So there is general babble, and soon I find myself saying, Rosalyn, *I* shall play for *you*. I sit down, and stumble my way through the saraband from the *First* Partita, after which I breathlessly ask her if she is familiar with Anatole France's *Our Lady's Juggler*, which to my dismay she is not; so I tell her about the monk—the ex-circus hand—who, having no relevant skills, and having observed the artful oblations rendered by his gifted brothers on the Feast Day of the Virgin, was spotted, late that night, standing before her statue juggling his five weatherbeaten circus balls; and she gets the point.

(Sunday, at the lunch to which Pat invited the painter, in exiguous expiation for the blood Foo had shed, he said to me that it was not until the next morning that he had completely focused on the spectacle of *my* playing the piano for Tureck; and we laughed, I more nervously than he, struggling, through the hoots of the company, to make the subtle but steadfast point that

144

what I did was only excusable in the light of the utter awfulness of my piano-playing. I recently showed one of my paintings to Marc Chagall, something I would never have done to a freshman art-instructor.)

We laugh on, and after a while I invite Rosalyn to my upstairs study, sit her down, and play her, on my brand-new Sony, a recording of the *English Suites* done by her, and we adore it together. Then I put on another record, done by another artist, of the same music, and we wince together, in which we are joined, presently, by the painter, the lawyer and his wife, and my wife, all of us crowded into the little room. I make one more pass at Rosalyn, hoping to seduce her one more time to the piano, but this time I fail. We giggle down the staircase, collect the coats, and tuck our guests into Rosalyn's waiting limousine. A wonderful evening. Worth the hell Pat gives me, made tolerable only because late though it is, vinous though our condition, I can still draw foggily on the resources of the debater, which I do by haughtily, and indeed just a *little* sadly, reminding her that Horrible Foo has, as, Catonically, I had always warned her he would, proved to be a wicked, wicked dog.

SATURDAY. Very unusual, a Saturday morning in New York. We sleep late, and send out for the New York *Times*, which is not delivered to 73rd on weekends. I make my way through it, without any sense of pressure, patting Foo ostentatiously under Pat's glare; and then to my study, and correspondence.

A gentleman from my home town of Stamford is cross,

reacting against my defense of Jim, which was written in the form of a letter to the New York *Post* a day or two before the election, and attempted to answer the attack on him by Pete Hamill.

I note that you often use an expression such as "he doesn't really suppose he thinks he exists" [I *hope* I have never used such an expression] or something to that ridiculous effect and I suppose you think that that is the epitome of sarcastic wit but you are mistaken because in reality it is you who do not exist because you are a phony from top to bottom hence why you are so distasteful to so many people besides the "liberals". Your politics—plain, old, ugly reactionary politics, just what do you think is so new about that, it's the oldest politics in the world. Your life style—a mick masquerading as to what you probably fantacize [sic—and hencefoward, sic] as being how an upper class Englishman lives. I have lived in England and Europe and believe you're just as upper class as Spiro Agnew, in spite of your frilly facade. Your pretence to religiosity—hypocritical something you have in common with that other phony Richard Nixon. . . . And as to your observation on knee-jerk liberals, you should talk, what are you but a knee-jerk reactionary with the emphasis on jerk. . . . Your frantic anti-communism is part of this knee-jerk reaction, you despise communist dictatorships, but the fascist ones are perfectly all right, also standard thinking to a right winger. Why you have been described as brilliant is really beyond me, you fit the pattern of any right wing group that has ever existed

146

in this world. As to my earlier reference as to your masquerading as an upper class Englishman, I am not an anglophile by any means but an original is always preferable to the fake, always. The people who lick your boots are frightened, people who do not have the intelligence nor the comprehension to see through your facade of good manners, affected vocabulary, and pretences to see you for what you really are, but as Abraham Lincoln said, "You can fool some of the people [the balance of the quotation was accurate]." That should give even such a brilliant wit such as yourself pause for thought.

Well, that is an ice-breaker, as Wilfrid Sheed once commented when I told him that on first meeting Ayn Rand she had looked me square in the eyes and said, "You ahrr too intelligent to beleef in Gott!" On the whole though, routine, except for the English bit. That comes up from time to time.

. . . I remember as a junior at Yale visiting in Omaha with my prospective brother-in-law Brent Bozell, whose home was there, and stopping at a roadside stand to buy a kite, only to find, when we attempted to fly it, that the package contained a mere 50 feet of string, which I thought unreasonable. So I drove back to the vendor, and made my complaint in what I thought a perfectly straightforward way, to which the proprietress replied, "Why don't you get out of here with your phony British accent?" I wish I had rolled off one of those nice squelchers that begin with "Madame," but I was simply flustered, to Brent's huge delight, and comforted myself that no one who *knew* England could confuse my "accent" with a British accent, although whatever it is that I do do when I speak is, apparently, slightly different. Yet here is a correspondent who has lived in England who thinks my elocution British. In the Army, at basic training in Georgia, I was simply thought of as Yankee, but even so, I found myself worrying then, at age 18, about the possibility of affectation in speech, and I wonder now why it is that my sister Jane, immediately older, and Trish, immediately younger, are never reviled by kite-vendors, or correspondents-at-large. We should have come out sounding alike; we had identical experience as children.

Years ago I wrote on the general subject of word-slurring—without reference to my own peculiarities. I recalled that I had recently spent the better part of a day with a college student who had much on his mind to tell me, which I looked forward to hearing. But after an hour or so I gave up. It wasn't that his thinking was diffuse, or his sentences badly organized. It was simply that I could not understand his words. When they reached my ear they sounded as faint as though they had been forced through the wall of a soundproofed room, as garbled as though they had been fed through one of those scrambling devices of the Signal Corps.

"Somi iggi prufes tometugo seem thaffernun."

"What was that?"

(Trying hard) "So me IGGi prufes tometugo seem THAafternuun."

"Sorry, I didn't quite get it."

(Impatiently): "SO MY ENGLISH PROFESSOR TOLD ME TO GO SEE HIM THAT AFTERNOON." And on with the story, by which time, let us face it, the narrative has become a little constipated; and soon I gave up. My responses became

148

feigned, and I was reduced to harmonizing the expression on my face with the inflection of his rhetoric. It had become not a dialogue but a soliloquy, and the conversation dribbled off.

It isn't a purely contemporary problem. Two generations ago Professor William Strunk Jr. of Cornell was advising his student E. B. White to speak clearly—and to speak even *more* clearly if he did not know what he was saying. "He felt it was worse to be irresolute than to be wrong," White reminisces in his introduction to *The Elements of Style*. "Why compound ignorance with inaudibility?"

I remember when I was growing up, sitting with my brothers and sisters at the dining room table in Sharon and making those animal sounds which are understood only by children of the same age, who communicate primarily through inflection. One day my father announced, after what must have been a singularly trying dinner, that exactly *four* years had gone by (hyperbole was his specialty) since he had been able to understand a *single* word uttered by any one of his ten children, and that the indicated solution was to send us *all* to England—"where they *respect* the English language and teach you to OPEN YOUR MOUTHS." We put this down as one of Father's periodic aberrations until, six weeks later, the entire younger half of the family found itself on an ocean liner headed for English boarding schools.

Mumbling was a lifelong complaint of my father, and he demanded of his children, but never got, unconditional surrender. He once wrote to the headmistress of the Ethel Walker School, "I have intended for some time to write or speak to you about Maureen's speech. She

149

does not speak distinctly and has a tendency, in beginning a sentence, to utter any number of words almost simultaneously. Anything the school can do to improve this condition would be greatly appreciated by us. I have always had a feeling [here Father was *really* laying it on, for the benefit of his children, all of whom received copies of his letter] that there was some physical obstruction that caused this, but doctors say there is not."

Frustrated by the advent of the Second World War and the necessity of recalling his children from England before they had learned completely to OPEN THEIR MOUTHS, my father hired an elocution teacher and scheduled two hours of classes every afternoon. She greeted her resentful students (it was during *summer vacation!*) at the initial class with the announcement that her elocution was so precise, and her breathing technique so highly developed, that anyone sitting in the top row of the balcony at Carnegie Hall could easily hear her softest whisper uttered onstage. Like a trained chorus—sitting a few feet away—we reacted: "What did you say? Speak up!" WE DID NOT GET ON. But after a while, I guess we did start to OPEN OUR MOUTHS.

No doubt about it, it is a widespread malady—like a bad hand, only worse, because we cannot carry around with us a little machine that will do for our voices what a typewriter does for our penmanship. The malady is one part laziness, one part a perverted shyness. Perverted because its inarticulate premise is that it is socially less obtrusive to speak your thoughts in such a way as to require the person addressed to ask you to repeat what it was you said. A palpable irrationality, as E. B. White suggests. If you have to ask someone three times what did he say, and then, after deciphering it, you come upon Hope's diamond, you will have the glow of pleasure that comes from knowing that the effort was worth the tribulation. But if at the end of the mine shaft you are merely made privy to the intelligence that the English professor set up a meeting for that afternoon, you are entitled to resent that so humdrum a detail got buried in an elocutionary gobbledygook which required a pick and shovel to unearth.

But all that is to sidestep the animadversion of my correspondent, whose complaint isn't against elocutionary clarity, but against a pseudo-English pronunciation. Or are they, in some people's minds, fused? Anyway, John Kennedy, with his very very broad a's, diminished the utility of "an English accent" used as a pejorative. It happens to be true that I learned to speak English in England, six years before Father sent us back there for more of the same. In 1932 my father moved his family from Paris to London. I arrived, age 7, speaking only Spanish, and a little French. But the tribal instinct quickly took hold, and I felt ashamed. I remember that the very first sentences I was rehearsed in at Blessed Sir (now St.) Thomas More's grammar school in London, were, "Oh Toby, don't roll on the road!", and, "How *now*, brown *cow!*", the mimicry of my earnest rendering of which, in a morganatic blend of low Spanish and high English, greatly amused my older brothers and sisters, and greatly pained me. Very soon after, we were back in Connecticut, and I strained to speak like Mortimer Snerd, so as to disguise from my friends the ignominy of my foreign experiences. The fashion is to comment on the hauteur of my diction. "After a late-show television appearance, an emcee may importune [David] Frye to reveal the man inside, and he always retreats into an impersonation," a current magazine story reports. "The eyes brighten and he becomes a serenely confident William F. Buckley Jr., darting out his tongue and wheeling his eyes and speaking in that tone of exquisite aristocratic dismay: 'Ahh, Mayor Daley, is, of course, the kind of guy I'd be proud, ahh, to call Daddy.' Frye comes over perfectly as Buckley and in the general delight generated by this fast act the search for the real Frye is forgotten." . . . To say nothing of the real Buckley.

John Leo, a few years back, when I was running for mayor of New York, did a New York *Times Magazine* piece on me and brushed up against the subject. I told him that I thought the hauteur so often remarked was probably a defensive intonation (adduced against an intellectual community I had come across first at Yale and have wrestled with ever after) which proceeded on the assumption that "conservatives" were simply, well, simpletons. I don't know, the reasoning is a posteriori, but the explanation is, even then, plausible. And of course its effects *can* be devastating. Ten years ago the publishers decided to bring out a new printing of *McCarthy and His Enemies*, which I had written, with Brent Bozell, during the general excitement of the McCarthy years, and I was asked to do a fresh introduction. I took the occasion to reminisce about the original edition, and the dour reception it received. "Mr. Dwight Macdonald, with his characteristic bounce, wished away our research [in *Partisan Review*] with the amusing comment that this book gives 'the general effect of a brief by Cadwalader

Wickersham and Taft on behalf of a pickpocket.' Like that of most of McCarthy's critics, here and abroad, Mr. Macdonald's position on McCarthy reduced to, 'I say it's spinach and the hell with it.' Not for years had there been a more sundering political controversy. Friendships were shattered—including, incidentally, mine with Macdonald. Six years went by before we met again, having been brought nervously together by a common friend. The lunch went well and through three courses the matter did not come up. But Macdonald could never turn his back for very long on Gomorrah, and abruptly he turned on me: 'You know, you *never* understood the real *evil* of McCarthy.' 'No,' I said, 'I never did.' He *laughed!* That is a good sign, isn't it?" . . . Teddy White, assigned by *Life* to the task of doing a piece on the great practical-intellectual thought leaders of America, asked to see me, not because he thought to include me among them, but because he wondered what a "conservative's" observations on the subject would be. So I told him (this was in 1966) that American conservatives were, very simply, unused to winning any practical-theoretical battles, thus we had nominated Goldwater, and Goldwater had lost triumphantly; that therefore our psychological posture tended to a resigned condescension towards the victors, whose political-intellectual dominance we protest only in the way that an embattled but philosophically secure opposition registers its protests against the intrenched mismanagers of the common destiny, impassionately, every now and then, when great events challenge us; but, rather than not at all, perfunctorily, resignedly. I remember being told about the weatherbeaten reactionary congressman, grown prematurely old by the fiscal

153

prodigalities of the New Deal, semi-paralyzed by the Hundred Days, who did nothing at all during his long career except to rise, a dozen times during each session of Congress, to make, wearily, the single observation, just prior to the passage of yet another expensive bill, "Gentlemen, where are we going to get the money?" It is the redeeming end to the story that toward the end of his life he rose, creakily, demanding the recognition to which the parliamentary rules entitled him, even though it was very late at night, at the point when a fatigued House of Representatives was prepared after days and nights of debate to pass the Lend-Lease Bill. The exhausted legislators groaned as the Speaker recognized him, just after midnight on the first of April, 1940. "Gentlemen," he said, "April Fool!" Just so, if conservatives ever actually take power—say as unexpectedly as Jim took the senator's seat in New York—they will have a great deal to worry about in the area of recovering their practical self-assurance. Meanwhile, they will be dismissed as simpletons; or, as haughty, or aristocratic; or, if they complain too loudly in the outskirts of Omaha, as phony Englishmen.

I do not answer my correspondent from Stamford. I think at first to do so, but the pile of mail is high, and in any case I don't see in his abusive letter either one of the two things I do not resist—a trace of a) geniality, or b) wit . . . A dentist from California writes to congratulate me on defeating John Kenneth Galbraith in the debate at the Cambridge Union, televised in America a week or so ago. "It must be very gratifying to have had the Union side with your arguments. It's somewhat like having the zoology, geology, and paleontology departments of the

remember that their first loyalty is to Him, and that conservatism is only a secondary crusade. At one time, totally ignorant of true Christianity as presented in the Bible, I thought that conservative principles, faithfully followed by elected officials, could in and of themselves revolutionize the world. I now realize, to my chagrin, that this belief—held by so many of my conservative friends—is just as much a thought towards the "immanentizing of the eschaton" as is any dictum passed down from the ivory towers of doctrinaire liberalism. As [Whittaker] Chambers so lucidly said, "Charity minus the Crucifixion is liberalism." In the same sense, conservatism minus the Gospel is unjustified bravado and plastic courage. Which leads to self-righteousness of a kind not seen since the Pharisees—as witness a certain lady [Ayn Rand] whose "philosophy" was devastated by Chambers in the pages of your magazine, and whom I fanatically followed before meeting the Living Lord . . .

Mr. Buckley, you have been extremely kind to me in the past, in giving me encouragement when I needed it, and in giving me love when I had finally seen the light of Calvary. Your letters meant more to me than you will ever know. At present, my activities include a good deal of writing for Christian magazines, and a good deal of work on high school and college campuses with Campus Crusade for Christ. However, a very great portion of my day is spent in prayer (I have found it necessary for survival), and my prayers are often with you. I no longer see you as "William F. Buckley, the Hope of

159

Intellectual Conservatism, the Heir to Burke's Throne." No, I see you now as a fellow-Christian, and a man—with all the frailties of dust, but who, according to the Bible, was made "a little lower than the angels." Should you lose your gift of eloquence, renounce conservatism, and man the barricades, my feelings for you will not have changed—because my own Saviour had you in mind when He hung naked and flayed on the Cross. My prayers are with you, no matter what transpires, and you have my love, whether you are ever aware of it or not.

Such a letter reminds me of how infrequently one finds the journalistically relevant opportunity to make a simple profession of faith—of how overbearing fashion is in these matters. Who, for instance, can remember a single utterance, by Robert Kennedy, say, concerning his faith in Christianity? I mention Kennedy without aspersion of any kind—on the contrary; because his foes and his friends agreed that he felt deeply, and it is at least the public understanding that he was not merely a practicing Catholic but a believing Christian. And he was not afraid to avow his passions, his idealisms. But would he have thought it, well, *proper*, to cite the passage above from Benjamin Franklin, let alone from a more orthodox Christian? The best I have ever done (not counting my book on Yale, which was in part devoted to documenting the studied disparagement of religion in the curriculum), is to be on the prowl for opportunities to *notice* the *existence* of Christianity: such an opportunity came for instance a year or so ago . . .

The doings of The Beatles (I wrote from London) are

minutely recorded here in England and, as a matter of fact, elsewhere, inasmuch as it is true what one of the Beatle gentlemen said in 1966, namely, that they are more popular than Jesus Christ. It is a matter of considerable public interest that all four of The Beatles have gone off to a place called Rishikesh, in India, to commune with one Maharishi Mahesh Yogi.

The reigning chic stipulates that Mysterious India is where one goes in order to Have a Spiritual Experience. Accordingly, The Beatles are there, as also Mia Farrow, who, having left Frank Sinatra, is understandably in need of spiritual therapy; and assorted other types including, the press reports, a space physicist who works for General Motors. It isn't altogether clear what is the drill at Rishikesh, except that—and this visibly disturbed a couple of business managers of The Beatles—a postulant at the shrine of Mr. Yogi is expected to contribute a week's salary as an initiation fee. A week's salary may not be very much for thee and me, but it is a whole lot of sterling for a Beatle, and one gathers from the press that the business managers thought this a bit much and rather wish that The Beatles could find their spiritual experience a little less dearly.

The wisdom of Maharishi Mahesh Yogi is not rendered in easily communicable tender. It is recorded by one disciple that he aroused himself from a trance sufficiently to divulge the sunburst, 'Ours is an age of science, not faith,' a seizure of spiritual exertion which apparently left him speechless with exhaustion. It is reported that The Beatles were especially transfigured when the Maharishi divulged, solemnly, that 'speech is just the progression of thought.' One can assume that the apogee

161

of their experience was reached upon learning, from the guru's own mouth, that 'anything that comes from direct experience can be called science.' It is a wonder that the entire population of the world has not gravitated towards the cynosure capable of such insights . . . (And then my pitch—)

I am not broke, but I think that if I were, I would repair to India, haul up a guru's flag, and—I guarantee it—I would be the most successful guru of modern times. I would take The Beatles' weekly salary, and Mia Farrow's, and the lot of them, and I would come up with things like—listen . . .

"Put on therefore, as the elect of God, holy and beloved, bowels of mercies, kindness, humbleness of mind, meekness, long-suffering; forbearing one another, and forgiving one another, if any man have a quarrel against any; even as . . . forgave you, so also do ye. And above all these things put on charity, which is the bond of perfectness. And let the peace of God rule in your hearts, to the which also ye are called in one body; and be thankful." To the especially worldly, I would say: *"Walk in wisdom toward them that are without, redeeming the time. Let your speech be always with grace, seasoned with salt, that ye may know how ye ought to answer every man."* Can it be imagined that I would be less successful, quoting these lines from a single letter of St. Paul, than Maharishi Mahesh Fakir has been? The truly extraordinary feature of our time isn't the faithlessness of the Western people; it is their utter, total, ignorance of the Christian religion. They travel to Rishikesh to listen to pallid seventh-hand imitations of thoughts and words they never knew existed. They will go anywhere to experience spiritually—

162

except next door. An Englishman in search of a spiritual experience need go no farther than to hear Evensong at King's College at Cambridge, or high mass at Chartres Cathedral; or read St. Paul, or John, or the psalmists. Read a volume by Chesterton—*The Everlasting Man, Orthodoxy, The Dumb Ox*—and the spiritual juices begin to run, but no; Christianity is, well—well what? Well, unknown . . .

That kind of thing is better done, by far, by Malcolm Muggeridge; but notice—*have* you noticed?—the smiles of condescension when, as so often it does, the Christianization of Muggeridge comes up in conversation? Bringing to mind the awful accuracy of Canon Bernard Iddings Bell's observation, twenty years ago, that to the extent that Christianity is suffered in the modern world, it is thought of simply as "an innocuous pastime, preferred by a few to golf or canasta." My guest is here, and I go downstairs to greet Otto von Habsburg.

I have known him, off and on, for quite a few years, and he has once or twice written for *National Review*, usually in defense of de Gaulle, whom, he insisted, we diligently misunderstood. He is technically the heir to the thrones of Austria and Hungary, though he had to renounce his claim to the Austrian throne in order to enter Austria, from which he had been exiled. He lives now in Bavaria with his large family, and makes his living as a journalist, author, scholar, and lecturer (in six languages). He is tall and thin, balding and mustachioed, and there is a trace of sadness in his courtly movements. He is a man of startling good manners, rising even when you re-enter the room, declining to sit down until you have yourself done so, yet accomplishing it all without giving off a drillmasterish pall, or appearing in any way unnatural. I sense that he has something concrete on his mind to discuss because at the time we fixed the date, many weeks ago, he prolonged his return to Austria by one day in order to fit in the lunch.

We chatter along—his grasp of the politics of almost every country in the world is extraordinary—but we do not come to grips with any single subject. Until I mention, over coffee, the estimate given to me last spring in Yugoslavia: that in the event the Russians attempted to overrun the country, Yugoslav guerrillas could, with what the militia now knows, tie down a million Russian soldiers indefinitely; after all hadn't they, under more straitened circumstances, tied down one-half million Nazi troops during the entire war? He contradicts me sharply. The difference, he points out, is this: the resistance, during the Second World War, harmonized with forces *outside* Yugoslavia which were determined to conquer the Nazis and had the resources to do so. That is what kept the resistance alive. No, he said, it won't be that way when, as is probable not long after the death of Tito, the Russians, opportunizing on the inevitable regional strife within Yugoslavia, decide to extend the Brezhnev Doctrine, and overrun Roumania, Yugoslavia, and, while they are at it, Albania. Yes, there would be resistance, but inasmuch as it is predictable that the West would not go to war to help Yugoslavia, and that nothing short of the threat of war would stay the Russians, the prospects for Yugoslavia are gloomy.

I ask after his flight, since it is now three-thirty, and he rises, telling me that he expects that his car is now waiting for him outside. We go out together, the car isn't there. He insists that he will wait alone for it outside my door, which is preposterous. So we walk around the block, and find, on returning, an enormous Mercedes limousine, which he busily assures me is not his, but a friend's who has obligingly put it at his disposal. We shake hands again, warmly, he is a lovely man. I still do not know whether I have been vetted for some specific purpose, but I did receive, a few weeks later, a letter from Otto, asking whether I would join a very small organization that meets two or three times a year, in Europe usually, but sometimes in America, to discuss deeply, and off the record, public policies affecting the future of the West.

Back to my study. Several months ago two men, one of them Pat Moynihan's brother, approached me asking if I would write directly to Colonel Papadopoulos to intercede in behalf of a Greek editor, cousin to the second of the men who came to my office. He has been sentenced to several years in prison not even for calling for the regime's overthrow in his newspaper, but for violating what struck me as an insubstantial part of the junta's censorship law. Why me? Because Colonel Papadopoulos could not suspect that I was a Communist plot. I told them that two years earlier I had been greatly amused, on being presented to Papadopoulos in Athens, at hearing from him, during the fifteen minutes we spent together, a sermon on the evils of Communism. I remember that he seemed smug, yet somehow a little unsettled. The papers that morning reported that in the wake of the general strike in France, President Charles de Gaulle had suddenly left the country for Germany—to resign, it was surmised; in fact, it transpired, he left in order to nail down the French army's loyalty, which he succeeded in doing at the price of promising amnesty for the generals and colonels still in jail for their revolutionary opposition to de Gaulle's Algerian policies a few years earlier. Papadopoulos referred contemptuously to the effects of the breakdown of even such a stabilized democracy as Charles de Gaulle had written into the constitution of the Fifth French Republic; but Papadopoulos could not know—nobody could know during those few days—just what it was that was going on in France; and might it—as in 1848—sweep the whole of Europe? Indeed, the world? Four days later Robert Kennedy was shot down.

Anyway, Papadopoulos has not replied, as I expected he would not, and the question now is, should we try other approaches? I write to Mr. Moynihan, to ask his advice . . . A letter from Corinna Marsh, whom I have never met. She is rumored to be 80 years old, in which case I cannot imagine what she did to her correspondents when she was 20. She is a tireless liberal, but writes always with a wink in her eye that softens her militant indignation. And she will acknowledge trans-ideological decencies, which just every now and then—rarely, but occasionally—she discerns in me, and mine. "Before I say anything else, I must and do congratulate the Buckley family on Brother Jim's victory, although [she will not even allow herself to end the sentence, and postpone her misgivings until the next one. That would suggest APPEASEMENT!] it does sadden me that such a 'moderate and cultivated man' owes his election so largely to immoderate and uncultivated members of what I am pleased to call the Stupid Majority. I do wish (as I

166

wished in re Stevenson when he ran against Eisenhower), that the *quality* of votes could be weighed instead of merely the percentages. However, I suppose the Republic will survive and I do congratulate the Buckleys on what I'm sure you consider a patriotic triumph. (Ah, sincerity, what sins have been committed in thy name!) Ambivalently yours, Corinna" . . . Julie Kenner, daughter of the author and critic Hugh Kenner, will be graduating from college in June, and is interested "in virtually any job in the journalism or publishing fields." I ask her to be a little more specific, and suggest that if she desires practice in writing, *National Review* is not a good place to go, because our stuff is, with the exception of the editorial pages, written outside the office, giving little scope to beginners . . . A graduate student doing a master's thesis on Orestes Brownson, whom he obligingly identifies, "(1803-1876), an American political philosopher well recognized by his contemporaries as an outstanding contributor to American intellectual life in the 19th century," needs financial aid. I write and ask him to answer the questions the Projects Committee of the American Historical Research Foundation, of which I am chairman, will want the answers to . . . A kind and literate and witty vice president of a San Francisco advertising firm writes me, in reply to a question about the difficulties *Firing Line* has in getting commercial sponsors.

First, by way of responding, an anecdote. Perhaps four years ago, when I occupied a lower position in our corporate hierarchy, I suggested to management that our company underwrite the cost of Firing Line for our local educational station. As I recollect, this cost was $300, which entitled the underwriter to a fair-sized plug both fore and aft of the hour. I argued that such an expenditure made good business sense in light of the quality of the audience and the favorable reaction it would doubtless provoke towards the underwriter. Management, which I would describe as Nixon-moderate with Agnew tendencies, was initially surprised that I, as the company's resident com-symp better-red-than-dead pinko, would even come forth with such a notion. I explained that a fundamental tenet of my Pinkoism was toleration and encouragement of other points-of-view, etc., etc., thereby unsettling them a bit more. Ultimately, this particular management group decided against the proposal, for the never-articulated reason that "Buckley's too damn controversial and even though we agree with most of his views, we don't think it makes good business sense to tell the world of our position." In other words, never never never take a public position, for fear of alienating a potential customer.

So be it. The point of the anecdote: businessmen in general seem to fear any overt alliance with matters controversial; and ad men in general seem to fear offending clients who have this fear. Hence, it's not often that an ad man says to his client, "Hey, Joe, I've got a great media idea. We'll sponsor Firing Line. Great ratings. Great cost efficiency. Great viewer involvement. Great. Huh? That's right. Yeah, Buckley's show. Gee, do you really think so? Sure. Whatever you say. Listen, Joe, no offense, huh, I mean. What are you doin' for lunch? I know a great place. Topless. Great." (Everything in American business is "great".) Now, this bit of paranoia is certainly hyperbolic, it's also my personal opinion, prejudice, hunch, whatever. Treat it as such.

American business. It was never obvious to me, when *Firing Line* began, why an advertiser who "associated" himself with it should be branded as sympathetic to *my* views, rather than those of my guests, who are, 95 per cent of the time, men with whom I disagree: but I resolved that the effort to get advertisements for *National Review* was quite enough to keep lit within me the general contempt I feel for the American businessman's efforts in the defense of American capitalism. ("The trouble with socialism is socialism," Willi Schlamm once observed; "the trouble with capitalism is capitalists.")

Although on the whole I find liberals a hardier, more daring breed, there are many among them who are ambushed if you test their theoretical approval of the ventilation of all points of view. I had fun with Arthur Schlesinger Jr. earlier this year: "Dear Arthur: I hope that Mr. Steibel [the producer of *Firing Line*] inaccurately reported a conversation with you concerning a proposed appearance on *Firing Line*. He told me that you declined to appear on the program because you do not want to 'help' my program, and you do not want to increase my influence, although to be sure you hope that the program survives. It seems to me that the latter desire is by definition vitiated by the initial commitment. If all the liberals who have appeared on *Firing Line* reasoned similarly, it would necessarily follow that the program would cease to exist—or is it your position that other liberals *should* ap-

169

pear on the program, but that *you* should not? And I should have thought it would follow from your general convictions that a public exchange with me would diminish, rather than increase, my influence. And anyway, the general public aside, shouldn't you search out opportunities to expose yourself to my rhetoric and wit? How else will you fulfill your lifelong dream of emulating them? Yours cordially."

The last was a fresh (rancid?) re-exploitation of the most unguarded sentence Schlesinger ever spoke. It was at a public debate with me, ten years ago, at which he spoke the words: "Mr. Buckley has a facility for rhetoric which I envy, as well as a wit which I seek clumsily and vainly to emulate." A year or so later I scooped them up, and stuck them, unadorned, on the jacket of my new book, and waited for all hell to break loose; which it did, telephone calls, telegrams, threats of a lawsuit. I saw Arthur at a party the next year, and told him that the deadline for the blurb for my *next* book was April 15, but that if he didn't have time to compose a fresh one, I'd use the old one, which was after all hard to improve upon. Arthur is my Alsop . . . My war against the irrational practices of the airlines is going very well. Three years ago, I got Eastern Airlines to offer wine on flights to Florida (they said the flight wasn't long enough, but that if I would fly Eastern to *El Paso*, I could have wine), and that was a tough one. It was war *à outrance*, with postcards to the president written from aboard National Airlines flights to Miami, while sipping National's wine. And then one day an *enormous* basket of delicacies arrived at my office, with the note, "We surrender—Eastern Airlines." My current war is with BOAC, which

170

decided that the only way to catch hijackers is to prevent passengers from coming aboard with more than a single piece of hand-luggage, no matter that you are willing to check in two hours ahead of time, giving BOAC officials ample time to remove the hand grenades from your brief-cases. I have won that one, my correspondent tells me . . .

The column on BOAC has elicited one of those rare acts of intellectual chivalry so seldom done, in the polemical world. It is from a well-known Harvard soci-ologist. "This is a long delayed fan letter, specifically oc-casioned by today's Boston *Globe* piece of how you transferred from BOAC to TWA and got your hand luggage on.

"I originally meant to write this letter maybe a year ago, when you reported Tom Hoving's blast at Vice Pres-ident Agnew in the name of an organization of which I was a Board member. Since he never informed *me* of that press release, and since it seemed to me to disagree com-pletely with the line of the organization, I resigned. This as you may see is rather more influence than most col-umnists have on their readers.

"A very long time ago, you may recall, [a Harvard colleague] and I wrote a footnote in which we made some silly psychological point about people on the right, and referred to you. Some time later, Frank Meyer brought me around to meet you at the offices of *National Review*, and I was truly embarrassed. I gave up psycho-logical explanations then and have never used them since. Even in talking of students and the New Left, tempting as it is, I now argue only with their ideas.

"This is really only a letter to tell you that an old lib-eral appreciates almost everything you write, and finds it expresses generally the best sense to be found in the Boston *Globe* (which, like so much else these days, seems to be half in the hands of the New Left). But I am suddenly reminded I have just published a book on my writings on students in recent years, recording my movement from a somewhat liberal to a somewhat conservative position, and since you may find it of interest, I am sending you a copy under separate cover." I thank him, inadequately.

The Young Americans for Freedom want to meet with me—either before or after the speech—next week, when I lecture at the University of Pennsylvania. "Should budgetary reasons necessitate it, please do not hesitate to call collect. Thank you." . . . A newspaper reporter who covered my own campaign in 1965 writes warmly, "I am looking forward to a party Jim is hosting tomorrow for the reporters who covered him during the campaign. It is typically thoughtful of him. I thought he got great press coverage, even from those who were hostile to his candidacy. I remember one *Times* reporter telling me one day, early in the campaign: 'I think it would be a disaster for America if this guy won . . . but he's one of the greatest guys I ever met.' I watched that reporter's stories carefully, and not once did he slam Jim. I expect Jim will continue to get a good press, because of his intelligence, honesty, and superior character. By the way, having interviewed your mother, I now know how you Buckleys came by your [good qualities]. Have a nice winter in Switzerland. Enjoy your skiing, and, as Mario Procaccino might say, don't fall down and break your ass." . . . And from a very old friend, in the Foreign Service: "I was in the U.S. on a special assignment and managed to hang on up there until after [Jim's] victory celebration in which

I was accompanied by an amazing number of colleagues. The joint is a hotbed of conservative subversion. The hard noses will get harder as we find political support. By the way, on my last assignment I was able, indirectly, to take the measure of RN's guts. He has got them. Thanks again for dinner and why don't you come down on a lecture tour to this lost continent. Chile is dead as I noted over dinner at your home some months ago. Several other countries down here are comatose. There is really no hope for South America and some benevolent neglect, spiked with a bilateral agreement with the USSR that there will be no missiles emplaced in South America, would seem to be a prudent policy." I write him that I plan to go to Latin America in January . . . A memorandum from Jim to his brothers and sisters addressed, as is his custom, and for the sake of economy, simply: "Siblings—I fear that recent events may result in periodic telephone calls to one and all by various members of the press, magazine writers, etc. Insofar as any such inquiries might have anything to do with me (or be attributed to me), I would like to suggest the following procedure. You may act on the assumption that no article or program has been authorized unless the fact is confirmed to you in advance by me or my press secretary, Mr. Leonard Saffir . . . I can only speak, of course, about stories which involve me or were triggered by my election. As a matter of policy, we would like to cool it at this time. Somehow or other, *Life* slipped through our defenses [a cover story on the family] but we hope others will not. In any event, you now have the excuse of having to refer to Len Saffir." . . . A friend sends me the masthead, clipped out of New York's premier pornographic

173

weekly, SCREW. "I don't know what can be done about this," he says in a covering card, "but wanted you to know." "This" turns out to be the listing of SCREW's publisher, as "Senator-elect Jim Buckley," which is apparently SCREW's favorite joke, it being the coincidence that the publisher is indeed someone called Jim Buckley . . . Mrs. John Dos Passos, whom I saw six weeks ago at her husband's funeral, writes on an early Christmas card, "Many thanks for your kindness and eloquence," the reference being, I imagine, to the obituary I wrote . . . The editor of the Philadelphia *Bulletin* desires me to meet the press before I speak at U of Penn, and to join him for dinner later with a few friends and his wife, a warm and amusing woman of apodictic opinions as regards the Use and Pronunciation of the English language. We will find that night to quarrel about the correct pronunciation of paradigm, which she says is pronounced paradim, and I say paradime, and it turns out we are both right, ho hum . . . From Minneapolis, a young man recently graduated from the University, who had been present in the audience when I addressed the freshman class four years ago, and heard my speech a fortnight ago. I had sent him my book on American conservative thought, *Did You Ever See a Dream Walking?* He thanks me for it. "About that speech, by the way, as usual, it took me 10 minutes to get on your wavelength. Unfortunately, from some comments I heard after the speech, it was obvious that quite a few people never even made the attempt, and yet these were the same who, predictably, were most vociferous in their criticisms. I myself was fascinated by the case you wove, particularly your use of the Founding Fathers' thoughts. To a person who listened carefully, and tried to

174

grasp the distinctions you made (some of them minutely subtle), it was a most rewarding evening. Although perhaps to some it appeared obvious, I was impressed by your analysis of the frustrations which much of Middle America feels, i.e., answering, or attempting to answer, the radicals' generalizations with data and other specifics." The letter would prove particularly heartening the next morning, when I turned to a review of the same speech delivered at Yale. But it is time to dress, and go out for dinner.

We arrive at La Seine more or less expecting that we will be dining alone with Truman Capote, but two other guests are there as we approach the table, a man and a girl, both of them tall and handsome. I recognize him, an anxiety crystallizing, as I recall our other encounter, a year ago. He and Pat had disagreed over Agnew, and Pat managed to scale her most objectionable heights, whence she takes to addressing her adversaries, "My good man," which is not the most endearing means of approaching Joe Fox, author and editor (of Truman Capote, among others)—causing, indeed, a certain tension. Well, here we are, and everybody kisses, or shakes hands with, everybody, and I do not catch, as so often happens, the name of the girl, who is young, slender, beautiful, and we sit down and order drinks. I find her a little formal; shy-type, I reason; but things move, as they tend to do with Truman, who is maybe a little bit officiously hospitable, acknowledging with his keen social intelligence that there is if not a mélange de genres—which he knows better than to contrive, unless he is feeling wicked, and this is not the night for that sort of thing—at least some im-

175

pacted static there, which he intends to dissipate, and succeeds in doing so, little by little. However Truman is not altogether himself, declining, for instance—though several times urged to do so—to dilate, as under normal circumstances he would do with vivacity and passion, on his recent highly publicized ordeal. Because he had followed—or because, I forget, he hadn't followed—his lawyer's instructions, he suddenly found himself on California's Most Wanted List for contempt of court. He had not appeared in court to give testimony on what it was that he knew, or didn't know, about a condemned prisoner whom he had interviewed in the course of producing a television special on capital punishment. Anyway, he has just come from spending ten or twelve hours in jail—a nasty resolution of judicial rectitude and executive agony, because the Reagans and Truman had become very good friends in the course of Truman's explorations into capital punishment. But it would have been unseemly for law-and-order Reagan to commute a celebrity-friend's five-day sentence. The strain of the experience is palpable, and although from time to time Truman rises buoyantly to describe this or that aspect of his tribulation, he doesn't want to recount what Joe especially wants him to tell us, and I sense that it pains him; so we let it go.

Along the way, the ladies go out to the powder room, and Truman tells me that the girl, who is called Lally, is the daughter of the late Philip Graham and of Mrs. Graham, now the publisher of the Washington *Post,* etc. —and that she was a bit hesitant about sharing an evening with me because she harbored a resentment over what I had published when her father died.

That column. *Time* Mag, when it did the cover on me, mentioned it. "In one breathtaking column, he managed to equate Henry Ford's divorce with the suicides of publisher Philip Graham and Stephen Ward, Christine Keeler's keeper. All were men, wrote Buckley, 'wanting in the stuff of spiritual survival.' Ford yanked its [projected] advertising from [*National Review*]." I tried to think back on what it was I had said, on whether I should be edgy about having said it; and I summon it up (while the ladies are out, in the fashion of John Fowles in *The French Lieutenant's Woman*). I remember writing it. It was mid-morning, drizzling, foggy, we were on my yawl, having left our anchorage at Campobello, just after dawn, in order to slide under the bridge at low tide, heading towards St. Andrews. I had to write a column and phone it in, so I turned on the radio to hear the morning's news ...

A single radio broadcast (I wrote) brings the news of two suicides and a divorce, and reminds us that, when all is said and done, it is the individual around whom the world spins. That all our talk of empires rising and falling, of worlds torn in two, of glacial currents and galactic swoops, can seem trivial when contrasted with the fall of a titan. The radio broadcaster relegated to the end the humdrum news of atom bombs, civil rights convulsions, earthquakes in Yugoslavia, tremors in the chancelleries. His mind and the listeners' were on the divorce of Henry Ford, the suicide of Stephen Ward, and the disintegration and death of Philip Graham.

All three were men of affairs in every sense of the word. All three men of rank. All three titans in their own worlds. Ford, the scion of a great fortune, perhaps the single most conspicuous figure in modern American industry. His forthcoming divorce, particularly under the circumstances of his voluntary and explicit commitment to a religion which holds that the marriage bond is unbreakable, involves a submission to an emotional impulse which proved overwhelming notwithstanding that the eyes of the world, which sustain many famous men in time of personal tribulation, were on him. Because, as the head of his fabulous empire, Ford was, like Rockefeller, not merely a scion of wealth and power, but a scion of manners, and manners in the deepest sense reflect the stability of civilization.

Stephen Ward, a successful physician, a talented artist, a gay and vivacious courtier, was dragged down to humiliation and despair and death by the whiplash of convention; and convention, let it be said in its favor, is in the profoundest sense the underpinning of civilization.

And poor Philip Graham, the most influential publisher in the most influential city in the world, lusting after the goods of mankind according to a defective vision which conceived of macrocosmic happiness following upon the rise of Big and Benevolent Government, couldn't, in the end, find his own happiness within his own circumstances, and suffered a nervous breakdown, departing despairingly from the world he had so fastidiously mothered by living and breathing the welfare state and international big-think. For himself, his own resources were overpowered; and it is on one's own resources, and God's, that each individual must finally depend, or else he and his civilization will disintegrate.

In two cases there was a woman. In the third, there was Woman. Over and over again there is the re-enactment of

178

Genesis, and the re-enactment of the causes of the down-fall of so many of the illustrious gods of Greek and Roman mythology, for whom woman is merely the sym-bol, not so much of man's weakness before the cunning and wiles of the seductress, but of man profoundly and primarily in love with himself. André Malraux wrote a great novel about a man of affairs, brilliant, worldly, ap-parently omnipotent, who sought women because through them he found the ultimate means of making love to himself: when he embraced women he was actu-ally embracing himself. The Protestant theologian Dean Fitch reminds us in his stunning book *Odyssey of the Self-Centered Self* that civilization has moved through several stages, and that we have recently entered upon the most acutely degenerate of them: The Age of Love of Self. For a period we loved God; then we loved rationalism; then we loved humanity; then science; now we love ourselves, and in that concupiscent love all else has ceased to exist. We are become what the philosophers called solipsists—men who recognize reality only in themselves. And when this happens, our own private lit-tle worlds, sustained only by our self-love, are easily shat-tered, and as they shatter we advance the destruction of our entire civilization, and race towards the Apocalypse ever so much faster than thermonuclear bombs will take us there.

The Greek dramatists knew that at the center of the weakness of the world is the weakness of the individual. How much we have forgotten in the 2,500 years from Aeschylus to Arthur Miller. The great heresies of recent times revolved around the repudiation of a plain truth. Marx instructed us that the fault lies not in ourselves but in history, that we are underlings, buffeted about by great elemental social forces which we do not dominate. Freud taught us that we should not blame ourselves for our failings, that other factors over most of which we had no control, traumatized and weakened us and made us impotent as superintendents of our own fate. The development of the philosophy of total welfarism is the political translation of the abandonment of the central idea of Christian civilization: that we are each one of us, however, crippled by burdens material and psychological, capable by the grace of God of working out satisfactory lives.

There was no misery or neglect in the development of the lives of Ford, Ward, and Graham; but they turned out to be the most miserable of men, men most seriously wanting in the stuff of spiritual survival; and because of their considerable names, they delivered considerable blows to the tattered wall of truth that stands between civilization and total relapse . . .

So. I think again of Wilfrid Sheed's comment "Well, *that* is an ice-breaker"; and I fantasize myself rising from my chair, when the girls come back, and solemnly recanting my column in atonement; and I recognize the singular cruelty to which such as Lally are subject, and wonder whether, under reversed circumstances, I would have difficulty in fraternizing with someone who had written thus about my father; and conclude that I would not:

I realize about myself that I am, for all my passions, implacably, I think almost *unfailingly* fair: objective, *just*. This is *not* vanity, it is rigorous introspection. I could not conceive, for instance, of disparaging another

180

man's talents simply because I disapprove the ends to which they are harnessed. Nor has this ever caused me any strain at all; indeed if it had done so, I'd be able to take such satisfaction as is due *only* to those who have to *struggle* in order to be fair. The ideologization of objectivity was brilliantly mocked by Randall Jarrell in his novel. "If [Flo] had been told that Benton College, and [her husband] Jerrold, and [her son] John, and [her daughter] Fern, *and* their furniture had been burned to ashes by the head of the American Federation of Labor, who had then sown salt over the ashes, she would have sobbed and said, at last—she could do no other—'I think that we ought to hear *his* side of the case before we make up our minds.' " That is the kind of objectivity that Kingman Brewster and the Yale students showed last spring, when they appeared to be taking the position that no murder should be investigated if there is the possibility that it was committed by a Black Panther. Not the same thing I am talking about.

And now, complacently, I cannot imagine that, reading them today, Lally, the daughter of a journalist and publisher, would find those heavy paragraphs polemically, or ideologically, horny. Still, I know that what is personally framed is more often than not personally received. A process that one once would have dared to call the feminization of criticism.

The coffee is waiting, and we drink it quickly, because Truman desires that we all should go to a place called The Sanctuary, way over on the West Side—a converted church, now a modish, super-hopped-up discothèque, psychedelic lights, blaring music, the dance floor crowded with homosexuals and lesbians and heteros, in ratio

181

about 25-25-50, who dance with detached expression: I conjure up a vision of the Archduke Otto and his Duchess, unsmiling, frugging there, calmly, serenely, doing as the Romans do—Imperial Breeding. For all the clamor, the participants are marvelously restrained; no one accosts Truman for an autograph, or begs him to read a manuscript. We are very nearly alone in ordering our whiskeys-and-sodas: everyone else seems to be drinking Cokes, or nothing at all. I suppose that they are also smoking pot, though I am not good at detecting the smell of it. Conversation is impossible, but Truman sits there, or dances with Pat or Lally, and he seems relaxed. I find the rock working through to me, not so much overcoming the resistance that is the conservative's presumptive protection against its licentious imperative as overcoming a different order of resistance: the resistance that collapses when one is cut off, almost absolutely, from any alternative to listening to it, or better, experiencing it. You can close your eyes at The Sanctuary and spare yourself conscription by the crazy-lights that focus, distort, slither, bump, propel, reject; but the music—the sound —is sovereign, and you do not talk; you dance or sit; and there is Truman sitting, his glasses occasionally refracting the light, his expression resigned, his face reposed, while the bodies, many of them black and beautiful, writhe, the faces always silent, resisting the inordinate, orgiastic demands of the sound: a total break with the tradition of audiences of The Beatles and The Rolling Stones. I think back on the night before, Rosalyn Tureck playing the saraband, the excitement that she caused, the strain with which one listens, concentrates to hear the little, noiseless, appoggiaturas, and the idea comes to me to write this

182

journal of a week's activity, and I wonder whether, tomorrow morning I will remember; whether anything will come of it if I do; whether anything worth the effort will come of it if I do.

It is late. We walk out into Truman's car, Lally and Joe get off first. We pick up the Sunday papers; Truman is chatting, entertaining us, the constant host, and he drops us at 73rd. We say good night and unlock the door, and Pat puts on the leashes and we walk Rowley, and Pepper, and Foo, and then go, silently, to bed.

SUNDAY. The idea of a week's journal has survived a long sleep's decompression, and in the quiet of a Sunday morning, when the telephone never rings, I give the project a little, a very little, hard attention, because I cannot think as the crow flies for very long, unless I am wrestling with somebody, or something, more viscous than my own runny thoughts. The ground rules. I like the idea of including *only* the activities of a single week. I remember being asked to do a profile of Murray Kempton for *Monocle* magazine's first (and very nearly last) issue. How to do a piece which even *attempts* to survey Murray Kempton's work? I hit on the device of writing "A Fortnight with Murray Kempton." I took eight consecutive columns by Murray, the eight that were published immediately before I embarked on the project. The essay was successful, I thought, because its limitations were at once explicit, and modest. I allowed myself to meander as I thought it useful. I shall apply the same rules, permitting myself to think back, when it seems useful, and even forward, as necessary. But I will attempt to

183

be disciplined (as distinguished from inflexible) in restricting the focus to people, problems, events, experiences, that have occupied me during this single week, which will end tomorrow.

A few little things. I am, in public situations, disposed to formality. On *Firing Line*, even if I have tutoyed them for decades, I always refer to my guests as Mr. or Mrs. or Miss So-So (indeed, a projected program with Kate Millett foundered on that psychological reef, because I told the producer that I could not agree to refer to her as "Kate"). I shan't do so here. "Mrs. Luce" will be Clare, that being how I address her. Then the name-dropping. I shall not affect unfamiliarity with those important people I happen to know, nor familiarity with those I do not happen to know.

Most difficult of all: how to handle the hyperbolic expressions of faith, or appreciation, or gratitude that are addressed to every public figure (and indeed to most private persons). Oh, yes, I am a public figure, there is no point in quibbling about that one. For one thing it is *res adjudicata*: the courts have so ruled. That is an amusing burden they imposed upon themselves quite recently, in *New York Times v. Sullivan*, the Supreme Court decision (1964) that says that if you are a public official you may not sue anybody for libel or slander unless you are prepared to establish that that person moved against you with "actual malice," which is defined as the saying about you of something which is in sharp contradiction of the known fact. A few years ago Linus Pauling sued *National Review* for calling him a fellow traveler. Our lawyers persuaded the judge that the reasoning of the Supreme Court in *New York Times* applied equally to public fig-

184

ures; and the higher courts sustained us. And, subsequently, hoist by my own petard, I have seen libelers try to excuse their scurrilities (what a wonderful word!) against me by pleading that I am a public figure, which the courts have acknowledged, leaving open the question (I have a case in mind) whether what was said about me was said with actual malice. Anyway, it would be a mistake at any level to suppress the hyperboles that cross my desk. That is the way they come in, in the mail, and, in such matters, a journal should be documentary, even as in the handling of the animadversions that come one's way.

Another thing. I determine, again for the documentary effect, to reproduce, rather than paraphrase, whole paragraphs as they crop up in letters to me, or in letters by me to my correspondents; or, in one or two cases, entire columns as I wrote them during this week or, in exceptional circumstances, as they crowd into the journal's narrative—rather than do the editorially more satisfactory paraphrase. Shall I always put them in quotation marks? Let the editor decide.

Again, is there anything at all to be done to leaven the self-centeredness of the enterprise? I fear not. It is launched, after all, as a most colossal effrontery: a public journal devoted to one's own thoughts and deeds over a single week. It must end as such, rather than attempt to squiggle into a demure extroversion.

And finally, is it possible in these circumstances to husband a little privacy? Yes—a precious little. My oblations to the muse I court are measured. I will make no effort to reveal everything about myself and my habits that might be of conceivable interest to the artist, to the prurient, or to the pathologist. And I shall not undertake to so much as mention, as I would feel required to do in writing an autobiography, such persons or events as have had made major emotional or intellectual impressions upon me. My father and my mother probably will not figure here, and my son is away. And so on. I shall try to execute the project during my Christmas vacation, in the Dominican Republic. I shan't succeed, of course, but I'll try.

So much for that. An hour or two, now, at my desk. The mail . . . An unpleasant clip from the *Yale Daily News*. After reading it I know that there isn't any point in trying to go on with my work, not until after I have composed an answer to it. That is Self-Knowledge. I know, also, that once I *have* answered it, I will feel as carefree as on leaving the confessional box, and though the memory will continue to be unpleasant, it will no longer nag me.

The story is headlined BRAYING THE BUCKLEY BLUES, the by-line is Hank Levine, who is introduced in bold-face type at the top of his story:

(Mr. Levine, a columnist for the *News*, is also chairman of the party of the Left of the Political Union. As such, he was seated next to Mr. Buckley during dinner at the latter's appearance before the PU [Political Union] last Monday.)

[And the story:] Beyond any reasonable doubt, there can be no experience more shattering to the nerves of a self-proclaimed young radic-lib than a confrontation with William F. Buckley, Jr. And

186

when the duel occurs at Mory's—closest thing to a Home Field that the editor of *National Review* could hope for at Yale—you early get the sinking feeling that any extended verbal battle with Bill is at best an orderly retreat in the face of overwhelming wit, and at worst a rout at the hands of the grand master of the devastating comeback.

I just went through the experience, and come away happy to report to fellow leftists that Buckley is not all he's cracked up to be. It is painful to lose an idol (we all worship the form, if not the content), and it is equally painful to gain a pompous bore, of which genre we have already a large surplus (especially on the *News*, Mr. Buckley would no doubt maintain).

I submit the following for Buckley admirers and critics everywhere.

• Mr. Buckley is charming. This is true—he has an easy grin, and though his manners leave much to be desired—he drank his soup straight from the bowl, without benefit of a spoon, and his elbows rarely left the table—he is altogether likable.

• Buckley's major form of comeback is a kind of silent leer-wince; both eyes shut tightly as thin lips twist into a semblance of a grin. Professor Rollin Osterweis, the archetype Old Blue, at one point early in the evening observed that all should shine in the dazzling glow of Buckley's reflected brilliance. The receipt of this paean modestly agreed that there was "plenty for everyone." At this point, I remarked through a fog of rising nausea that the large stock indicated an excess of supply over demand.

Wince . . . leer. . . silence.

Somehow, Buckley's silences always emerge as dramatic pauses—his oppositions' as pregnant gaps.

• Left to himself, Buckley could, in the immortal words of J. Breslin, "yell fire in a theater and put everyone to sleep." With a target to rebut, the man comes alive—if only long enough to leer and wince. Without one, he resorts to pontification and references to various dead people, all monotonic and delivered to his notes. Buckley spoke to the Political Union from Battell Chapel's pulpit, with an enthusiasm that would make Alfred Hitchcock look like a frenetic demon, by comparison.

• Politicians always evade questions. Buckley claims, with his favorite line "If it were true I'd tell you," that he is not a politician, but he evades questions anyway. "Mr. Buckley, how did you come to call John Lindsay a loser and talk of Conservative trends in 1969 when he got 42 per cent of the vote, but then call your brother a winner and discuss more Conservative trends when he got 39 per cent in 1970?" Grin . . . leer . . . "That's not exactly the way I phrased it . . ."

For all his finely tuned brains, Buckley at times has great difficulty reasoning his way through a paper flag. The speech I was privileged to walk out on was long and dull and deserted by a significant portion of the audience (rude, Buckley will claim . . . intelligent, we will answer). It consisted of several propositions each developed at length, but boiled down to a defense of the right of a Democratic state

188

to use "repression" or violent means against those who seek to do it harm.

Well and good and old as the hills. The chief example of this privilege of the state's was unfortunate —a defense of the Chicago 7 prosecutions. The defense was buttressed by quotations from the founding fathers, most notably that old monarchist, Alex Hamilton, who would doubtless be in prison for treason were he alive today.

Now, as most lawyers (including those employed by the Justice Dept.) read the law, you do not have to meet or act to be a conspiracy; you merely have to think disruptive thoughts—preferably the same as others are thinking—and intend to do something about them. Mr. Buckley claims liberals are muddying the Constitutional waters by interpreting certain sections (like the fifth amendment) too broadly, and ignoring others. He would do well to note that nowhere does the Document give Congress authority to regulate thought; that accordingly all thought (except for telepathic messages which cross state lines) is under state jurisdiction, and that therefore a true strict constitutionalist would fast slap down the Conspiracy law as a dangerous breach of law and precedent. I shan't (big Buckley word—shan't) even mention (perish the thought, especially if it is illegal) the idea that any Democratic state which seeks to violently restrict its citizens' thoughts is no longer Democratic and loses the "moral" rights to compel obedience with which it may have been endowed by that adjective.

189

Buckley tends to subjugate consistency to ideology. As a member of the advisory board of the U.S. Information Agency, he spent considerable time regaling us with his version of its aims. Uppermost in his mind was a desire that it be more independent from the State Department. State, to Buckley, is mealymouthed and overly conciliatory; he would prefer to see the USIA hit out a little harder at the Reds, not lying but selecting facts to publicize our better side and their worse side with a bit more fervor. Of course, independence is intrinsically good in any case. "Mr. Buckley, would you still favor that kind of policy independence if State were to start taking a 'hard line?' " Wince . . . leer . . . silence. As it was Mr. Buckley's birthday, we wished him many happy returns . . . to whence he came.

Letters-to-the-editor need to be brief, and no brief letter could possibly handle Levine's omnibus indictment. The instinctive thing to do is polemically probably the right thing to do. Smash him. (There is no time to treat him as Newman treated Kingsley.) Jules Feiffer, introducing a volume of hate-Johnson cartoons during the last months of LBJ's Presidency, made what I take now to be an artistic point. The "secret ingredient" of truly successful cartooning, he said, is *"hate.* Not personal hate, but professional hate: *the intensity of conviction that comes to a craftsman's work when he has made the decision to kill."* Now a lethal cartoon at the expense of LBJ may require the fodder of hatred. The put-down of an undergraduate—notwithstanding that you are here dealing with a dangerous enemy whose brawler's spirit has tri-

190

umphed over his technical callowness—cannot be fueled by hatred, however platonic. Even so, the Feiffer Rule is artistically useful. One must have the young man's head . . .

Where is his principal weakness? Not the constitutional or the theoretical arguments which, precisely because they are travesties, are unanswerable in a single paragraph. On the other hand they cannot be totally ignored; *some* assertion as to the quality of your argument must be there, somehow, lest you leave the impression that you are indifferent save to the personal insults. Point two: You can't defend yourself against subjective characterization: *That man is boring. That man is ugly. That man's mannerisms are distracting.* Hauteur is very, very useful; but careful, careful, it must not incline to pomposity, especially important when dealing with the kids. Citation of Authority can be useful, but you cannot *lean* on it. "Horowitz thinks I play the piano brilliantly" is dangerous, never mind whether you are gambling on the reader's forgetting that Helen Traubel once said that Margaret Truman sang brilliantly. It cannot be stated that directly, because the structure can collapse under a formulation so martial, even as they warned us, in the infantry, always to break step when crossing a bridge. "There are those who, after hearing me play, will perhaps side with Horowitz, rather than Levine, on the matter of my qualifications as an interpreter of Chopin" is more like it: leave out Horowitz's categorical encomium. So . . .

Dear Sirs: I have just seen the account by Mr. Hank ["Mr. Hank." I profit from the oxymoron] Levine of my visit to Yale a couple [be carefree] of weeks ago, and am constrained [you are exerting yourself towards benevolence] to comment on one or two of the things he said, and didn't say [important: This accounts for what you do not now accost].

1. When Mr. Levine approached me at the reception given by the Political Union, he announced himself as the Chairman of the Party of the Left. I replied that I admired such professions of humility. [Dans l'esprit d'escalier. On the other hand, no more had *he* said what he wrote he had said; or I what he wrote that I had replied.] He thereupon ventured something sycophantic [true: but I make it sound worse than it was], and I turned away the compliment with characteristic grace [I find it useful, here, to play the monseigneural role Levine assigns me], and resumed my conversation with Professor Rollin Osterweis, who happens to be an old friend. Apparently I greatly offended Mr. Levine, which it was certainly not my intention to do, because I have a very full schedule, and a very long waiting list. [Neat. The notion that to give offense is itself an act of recognition.]

2. I say apparently I did, because the next thing I read, after a strange distortion of my conversation with Mr. Osterweis (wherein a jollity we exchanged was treated with the solemnity of the Japanese surrender), was the criticism Mr. Levine made of my table manners. They "leave much to be desired." Indeed, "he drank his soup straight from the bowl, without benefit of a spoon." I suggest that the Party of the Left has finally found itself a Program: the redistribution of table manners. [The ideologization of his personal criticisms. And the sly imputation of snobbery to the socialists' program.] Why

192

should some people be allowed to have bad table manners, and not other people? Workers of the world unite to keep at least one elbow on the dining room table! [On this one, Mr. Levine is on the ropes.]

3. Concerning my address, those who are curious to know whether it could have been quite as jejune as Mr. Levine suggests may want to look at it. It is available in *The Great Ideas Today, 1970,* published by the editors of the *Encyclopaedia Britannica,* who apparently found it interesting [Horowitz is satisfied], which is not to say that it qualifies to interest those whose concerns are with . . . but with that aposiopesis [an artistic coup de grâce, I think, for someone who has accused me of making my points by grimaces] I take leave of you,

With most cordial regards,
Wm. F. Buckley Jr.

There now, and not a leer or a wince to sustain it. But a precaution. "Dear Doug [to the editor of the *Yale Daily News*]: It was pleasant to visit with you. Here is a letter. I'd appreciate it greatly if you would have someone you greatly trust copyread it. Nothing's worse than a little mistake in a tightly written thing. Newspapers, Hugh Kenner never tires of reminding me, are 'low definitional media' and therefore—as he puts it—it is unsafe to arrange your thoughts in such a way that the communication of them depends on the correct placement of a comma. But we can try, right? Right. Would appreciate your sending me a clip. By the way, *Who* put the fox in Hank Levine's bosom? If you like that, you may have it, free gratis, as the title for my letter on the Letters Page."

Another clip concerning the same speech. A New

Haven newspaper (speaking of Kenner's Law) has managed a distortion of quite extraordinary magnitude. "Buckley stressed, 'Such self-proclaimed revolutionaries as Hoffman, Rubin, Dellinger and Seale do not appear to understand the theoretical, let alone the practical, *tactics* of the counter-revolutionary.'" I said *rights*. "Claiming that the American Revolution of 1776 is the 'touchstone' of the new revolutionaries, Buckley added, 'It is instructional to remember that the British were entitled to *resent* it.'" I said *oppose* it. "He said the Hoffmans and Dellingers should be reasoned, laughed, and disdained into *ignorance*.'" I said *impotence*. A letter to the paper? God no.

That evening in New Haven had been, I thought, rather listless, beginning with the press conference at the *Yale Daily News*, in the Board Room where the picture of Britten Hadden hangs. He was chairman the year that Henry Luce was the managing editor. I was chairman in 1950. (A year or two ago, under the impulse of participatory democracy, the kids decided that the old set-up, based on an omnipotent chairman, should no longer be countenanced, so they formed a triumvirate: a business manager, a managing editor, and an editorial page director. Two years after triumvirization, there is dissatisfaction, and talk of reverting to the traditional arrangement.)

. . . I remember when we crowded into that Board Room for elections, in the early spring of 1948. I had asked Jim, who was in Law School, and who had served the *News* as an editor before the war, whether there was a tradition on the matter of voting for yourself for a particular office: i.e., was it gentlemanly for me to vote for myself (the ballots are secret) for chairman? He advised me—and on such matters Jim's advice is absolutely final —that he thought it okay under the circumstances, the circumstances being that at Yale the tradition used to be emphatically, indeed disqualifyingly, against any electioneering for any elected position whatsoever: you simply didn't do it. So, on that feverish afternoon, I had scribbled my own name on the ballot, and ten minutes later Sam Walker, the chairman of the preceding board charged ex officio with administering the election, came in from the antechamber with his assistants, to announce that I had been elected chairman. Pause. And he turned to me and winked: "Unanimously."

. . . We moved after the press conference to a reception in the quarters of the Yale Political Union, where so help me God the conversation did not go as reported by Mr. Levine. Then to dinner at Mory's, to which I had asked that two guests be invited, one of them a faculty member I had never met, but who had been in correspondence with me; the other my nephew Hunt, a freshman who graduated with my son Christopher from Portsmouth Priory last spring.

The young professor is a *conservative!* and had written me to ask if I would teach a seminar next fall at Yale, provided he could get the faculty to approve it. I had told him no, sorry, there is no time and he wrote: "About that course: let me say to what extent I am serious and in what extent not. Actually, I would like to get you up here once a week to do something—it's getting to the point where we can no longer hear the gadflies amid the clatter of falling idols. But I understand your reasons—time, money, etc. OK. That leaves two options: a) The sport of faking the project until it is turned down, hopefully by the Yale Faculty in solemn assembly. Delicious! b) And this is serious—a course in, say, 'Roots of Conservative Thought' (or whatever) run by someone (me and/or somebody else) in which you would promise to appear (and do a smattering of homework for on the train— nothing else) say just *six times*. You would be jointly responsible, officially, but not much actually. Fifteen students. Fall semester of next year. Definitely not to be a gut. And we'd still have the fun—a very serious but un-solemn sort of fun—of liberals being forced to check on their own liberality, in order to O.K. the course. (College [Yale College is composed of a dozen residential "colleges"] seminars are credit courses taught in the colleges and 'of an experimental or innovative nature.') Would you think about this?" "At this point," I replied, "I'm inclined towards a). The trouble with b) is that six times is too many times. Also, it has the disadvantage of not really establishing the formal point you seek to establish, to with my [ideological] disqualification to teach. After all, if I were merely a [classroom] exhibition, anybody would serve; the faculty could hardly object. In this re-spect, I will now sound a little bit traitorous by suggest-ing that you ought to consider that in fact I have no for-mal qualifications to teach. Sure, mine are as advanced as Eldridge Cleaver's, but he himself is controversial. I do not even have an M.A. So that it is not inconceivable that even conservative-minded professors could object on theoretical grounds to listing me as a member of the fac-ulty. Your thoughts?" At which point the professor sent a note saying that he would like to talk to me about it, so I

196

suggested he join the political chieftains at dinner at our forthcoming meeting at Mory's.

. . . After dinner they brought me a birthday cake, an extraordinary act of thoughtfulness, and then we walked to Battell Chapel, an unusual place to hold a political meeting—though maybe not; in recognition of which I began my speech by declaiming, "O Lord, ignore everything you have heard from this pulpit, from the lips of your humble servant, William Sloane Coffin Jr." And then, The Speech.

Number 3. Here it is. Beginning with the hated

PROPOSITION ONE: *The opinion-making community misunderstands the usefulness of repression.*

I mean by this proposition to draw attention to the great success that the recent mentors of American civilization have enjoyed when they suggest that repression is the kind of thing practiced only by storm troopers and rationalized in *Mein Kampf*; or, in other situations, by such as Lester Maddox in his chicken restaurant, driven by theories of white supremacy.

There is no evidence in early American history that I know of to suggest that the men who wrote the Constitution believed that all thought was in some way equal, simply because they went on to devise a Bill of Rights that forbade the Congress from enacting any laws abridging the freedom of speech or of the press.

When Thomas Jefferson spoke about the virtue of tolerating even those who seek to repeal our republican forms of government, it is clear from his other writings, and from the lapidary record of his

197

own activities, that what he meant to say was that the toleration of certain kinds of dissent is a tribute to the good sense of the American people who will always reject the blandishments of the anti-republican minority. So then, why interfere with the minority who wish to practice tyranny? It is, after all, a form of democratic self-confidence to be able to stroll peacefully through Hyde Park and listen to the orators who denounce our free institutions. It summons to mind the cozy child's dream, wherein you wake up suddenly in a jungle surrounded by wild beasts who however are powerless to harm you, because you are protected by an impenetrable bubble of glass which is proof against their aggressions.

Abraham Lincoln the polemicist pulled a fast one, Professor Harry Jaffa reminds us, when he began his Gettysburg Address by dating the beginning of the American Republic not with the Constitution but with the signing of the Declaration of Independence. His old adversary Stephen Douglas, during the famous debates, based his case on the Constitution alone—with exclusive reference to which it could indeed be argued that the Dred Scott decision was meticulously correct in forbidding the free-soil states from refusing a slave-owner the right to take residence there along with his slaves. Lincoln cited the beginning of the United States as having taken place "four score and seven years" before Gettysburg. That is to say in 1776, with the adoption of the Declaration of Independence. Accordingly—said Lincoln in effect—the metaphysics of the Declaration of Independence ani-

198

mate the Constitution, so that when scholars and statesmen disagreed—as they would do with progressive heat in the years that led to the explosion of civil war—on how to reconcile the postulates of America with the survival of slavery, it was to the Declaration of Independence that the abolitionists ideally repaired for guidance. Because the Declaration of Independence spoke of "self-evident" truths. Among them that men are born equal.

The initial toleration of slavery, in the understanding of Lincoln, was a historical accommodation. The accommodation of a great weight on America's neck: a birthmark. To be recognized by its leaders as such; so that step by step they might direct public policy towards emancipation by attrition. Professor Jaffa reminds us that "no American statesman ever violated the ordinary maxims of civil liberties more than did Abraham Lincoln, and few seem to have been more careful of them than Jefferson Davis." And then he adds the point which is so striking in the contemporary situation, *"Yet the cause for the sake of which the one slighted these maxims was human freedom, while the other, claiming to defend the forms of constitutional government, found in those forms a ground for defending and preserving human slavery."*

It is instructive to meditate on this apparent paradox at a moment when so much of the liberal community is disposed to denounce such modest little efforts as are nowadays being made to enhance the public order.

PROPOSITION TWO: *The absolutizers, in their*

199

struggle against what they call repression, are doing their best to make the Constitution of the United States incoherent.

It ought to be obvious that it is impossible to absolutize any single freedom without moving it into the way of another absolutized freedom. How can you simultaneously have an *absolute* right to compel testimony in your own behalf (Amendment VI), while others have the *absolute* right (Amendment V) to refuse to testify lest they incriminate themselves? How can you have *absolute* freedom of the press (Amendment I) alongside the *absolute* right to a fair trial (Amendment VI)? How can you have *absolute* freedom of speech (Amendment I) alongside other people's *absolute* right (Amendment XIV) to their property, including their good name?

Oliver Wendell Holmes, asked to define a fanatic, said something to this effect. Look, everyone will agree as a matter of common sense that a houseowner owns the space above his roof, such that, for example, he can legally prevent his neighbor from constructing a lateral extension reaching out over his own house. The fanatic, by contrast, will carry the argument forward absolutely. He will reason from his ownership of the space above his roof to ownership of a shaft of air that projects straight out into the heavenly spheres, such that no child's kite or supersonic transport can overfly him, without written permission. It is ironic that it is to a famous dissent of Oliver Wendell Holmes that the absolutizers (which is to say the fanatics) turn, when insisting that all ideas are to be treated with absolute impartiality. It was Justice Holmes who

200

said that "the best test of truth is the power of the thought to get itself accepted in the competition of the market." If that maxim were accepted, white superiority would long since have been accepted as truth in parts of this and other countries. In any event, the statement is hard to reconcile with the notion that some truths are "self-evident." Certainly it is hard to reconcile with the attitudes of the men who urged the adoption of the Constitution.

After all, the Federalist Papers stressed among other things the usefulness of a federal government in guaranteeing freedom within the individual states. Concerning the problem of indigenous threats to the republic, Alexander Hamilton wrote most directly. His plea for the proposed Constitution was not merely a plea against the anarchy that every schoolboy knows he abhorred. He warned also of the dangers of despotism. *"It is impossible to read the history of the petty republics of Greece and Italy,"* he wrote, *"without feeling sensations of horror and disgust at the distractions with which they were kept in a state of perpetual vibration between the extremes of tyranny and anarchy."* But he went on to argue that historical advances in the science of government now permitted the granting of powers sufficient to avoid anarchy, yet insufficient to promote tyranny.

Hamilton insisted that the government dispose of such power as is necessary to make its laws obeyed. Such power, it might be argued, the exercise of which the contemporary revolutionists, and their fellow travelers, are quick to criticize, invoking an absolutized version of the Bill of Rights.

Hamilton wrote in criticism of the Articles of Confederation that the government as then composed had *"no powers to exact obedience or punish disobedience to [its] resolutions, either by pecuniary mulcts, by a suspension or divestiture of privileges, or by any other constitutional mode."* Unless that situation were remedied, he warned, the United States would *"afford the extraordinary spectacle of a government destitute even of the shadow of constitutional power to enforce the execution of its own laws."*

So the Constitution that Hamilton and the others advocated was adopted; and inasmuch as it expressly guarantees republican government to each constituent state, we get a little historical focus on Thomas Jefferson's vainglorious boast about the nation's toleration of those who would tear down our republican forms of government. Hamilton went on—in his analysis—to commit the same sin of civic pride that Jefferson was to commit more flamboyantly a few years later; that John Stuart Mill would elevate to democratic dogma in a generation; and that Oliver Wendell Holmes took to the final extreme in 1919. Hamilton simply assumed that as a general rule a republican form of government would more or less predictably commend itself to the people, so as to make it obviously futile for a numerical minority to have any hope of repealing or frustrating it. He ambled along contentedly—up to a point—with the great syllogism that modern revolutionists are now bent on challenging, namely, that if the government is of the majority, there is no reason to suppose that there will be much latent support for revolutionary disruption. *"Where the whole power of the government is in the hands of the people,"* he said, *"there is the less pretence for the use of violent remedies in partial or occasional distempers of the State. The natural cure for all ill-administration ... is a change of men."*

But what about those situations in which republican government is threatened—whether by an assertive minority, or a passive majority, or a combination of the two? How much power should a government have in order to protect the republic against insurrection? A very important question, which is being fought out today in Congress, in the courts, and among the opinion-makers.

On this matter the absolutists—for instance, the American Civil Liberties Union—feel perfectly at home with all the old rigidities. But they are not winning *all* the constitutional debates. It is currently being tested, for instance, whether the government may punish those who, in the opinion of the court, conspired to go to Chicago for the purpose of abridging the freedom of others to transact their business at the Democratic Convention. Never mind, for the purpose of this analysis, the inflamed question: whether the trial judge behaved as inexcusably as the defendants. The question arises: Is the 1968 Act, under which the Chicago 7 were tried and convicted, constitutional? *"The idea of restraining the legislative authority, in the means of providing for the national defense,"* Hamilton ventured, *"is the one of those refinements which owe their origin to a zeal for liberty more ardent than enlightened."* He argued that, after all, *"confidence must be placed some-*

203

where," and that *"it is better to hazard the abuse of that confidence than to embarrass the government and endanger the public safety by impolitic restrictions on the legislative authority."*

So then, was Hamilton encouraging something which nowadays would go by the name of "repression"? *Precisely. "The hope of impunity is a strong incitement to sedition; the dread of punishment, a proportionably strong discouragement to it."* Over and over again Hamilton leans on the assumption that the general majority are as a practical matter going to be content with laws which are after all of their own devising. Nevertheless, Hamilton implicitly acknowledged that irrationality could now and again raise its ugly head. To assume that the government in a democratic society will not ever have to use force to assert its laws is naïve. *". . . the idea of governing at all times by the simple force of law (which we have been told is the only admissible principle of republican government),"* he writes acidulously, *"has no place but in the reveries of those political doctors whose sagacity disdains the admonitions of experimental instruction."*

Very well then, if we concede that the right to attempt to bring down the republican forms of government is not absolute, either in theory or in the historical experience of America, does it follow that we are bound to indulge, let alone applaud, such expressions of public impatience as for instance are embodied in the 1968 Act—which was the basis for the prosecutions in Chicago during last winter? We come to

PROPOSITION THREE: *Such self-proclaimed revolutionists as Messrs. Hoffman, Rubin, Dellinger and*

204

Seale, and such others as, for instance, Tom Hay-
den and William Kunstler, do not appear to un-
derstand the historical, let alone the theoretical,
rights of counter-revolutionists.

In the beginning—for our contemporary revolutionists—was the American Revolution. It is their
charter, the touchstone of their thought, their
polemic and their action. It is argumentatively as
important to the defense of their dogma and to
their behavior, as Prohibition is to the defense of
the young pot-smoker who says if the older generation could drink unconstitutional booze, why can't
we smoke illegal grass. The revolutionists insist
that this country was after all baptized in revolution, that revolution is genetically a part of the
American way.

I do not find anywhere in the informed literature of that period any suggestion that it was other
than the accepted right of the British throne to
resist the American Revolution. Edmund Burke,
whose sympathies were plainly with America,
never suggested that King George was violating
any known canon of civilization by sending a large
army to America to say No to the army of George
Washington. And if Washington had been caught
and hanged, Burke would no doubt have deplored
royal punctilio; but there was no higher law
around to appeal to than had been available to
Vercingetorix to use against Julius Caesar. By the
same token, the United States is entitled by all
conventional standards—to hang its revolutionists.

I should not think that the time to do this has
come, but certainly the time has come to remind
the revolutionists what are the possible consequences of their activity. As Dr. Johnson told us,

"The knowledge that you are going to be hanged in two weeks concentrates the mind wonderfully."

If then, the contemporary revolutionists can find no historical right to revolt against our society under immunity from repression, can they find any abstract "right" to commend their enterprise? The wording of the Declaration of Independence clearly shows the mark of the social-contract theorists. *"Governments are instituted among men"* in order *"to secure"* certain *"rights,"* said the Declaration. These governments derive *"their just powers from the consent of the governed."*

Here is an interesting distinction—obviously done in passing—between "just" and "unjust" powers; a tacit acknowledgment that even those governments that are licensed by the governed typically exercise both powers that are just and powers that are unjust. The contemporary revolutionist argues that those unjust powers the government exercises are not in fact intelligently sanctioned by the majority (Marcuse goes in for that kind of thing, in a tortured sort of way), but, rather, are institutional accretions. What is to be done about them?

Mr. Jefferson's Declaration of Independence acknowledges the *"right of the people to alter or abolish"* their government and *"to institute new government, laying its foundation on such principles, and organizing its powers in such form, as to them shall seem most likely to effect their safety and happiness."*

The Declaration goes on to enumerate the grievances of the colonies. It is a stirring catalogue, but it finally reduces to the matter of the *source of power*, i.e., *who* should rule? *"He* [King George] *has refused his assent to laws, the most wholesome and necessary for the public good,"* said the Declaration. Who is to decide what are the laws most wholesome and necessary for the public good? Why, the people—the people who are affected by those laws. The American Revolution was about *who* should rule. Everybody? Mr. Jefferson, perhaps from a sense of tact—perhaps even from a sense of cunning—introduces into the peroration of his manifesto a subtle distinction. *"We, therefore, the representatives of the United States of America, in general Congress assembled, appealing to the Supreme Judge of the world for the rectitude of our intentions, do, in the name, and by the authority of the Good people of these colonies, solemnly publish and declare . . ."* The *good* people of these colonies? A ritual obeisance? Or a sly recognition that there are plenty of colonials around who oppose secession? Bad people?

Mr. Jefferson always acknowledged the existence of bad people, in a way that Oliver Wendell Holmes had difficulty in doing, so absolute was his relativism. But Jefferson's rationalist's faith in the inherent power of good ideas to defeat bad ideas in the marketplace was ringingly proclaimed in his later years. *"Those who wish to dissolve the union or to change its republican form should stand undisturbed as monuments of the safety with which error of opinion may be tolerated where reason is left free to combat it."* It isn't of course suggested in this passage what is the indicated course of action if reason should fail in the performance of its delegated duty, but we know from Jefferson's own autocratic habits that he often gave reason a helping hand; and we know from the Declaration of Independence that he dubbed some truths as self-evident; and, derivatively, that he judged those people who acknowledged those truths, as "good," and those who did not—as something else. It was also Jefferson, presumably in a more skeptical frame of mind, who said, *Let no more be heard of confidence in man, but bind him down from mischief by the chains of the Constitution.*

From all of which one infers that in Jefferson's America, a) there is, on some very basic points, a right and a wrong position; that b) the probability is that the people will opt for the right position, prodded by reason to do so; but that c) it sometimes becomes necessary to resist the bad people, whether they are numerous, or whether they are, simply, the King of England. Abbie Hoffman is not the King of England, but the point of course is that he seeks a kind of metaphorical accession to the throne, by the use of any means, and the corollary point in our troubled times is: shall we restrain him, a); and if so, b), how; and c), how shall we protect not so much the White House from his occupation of it, but how shall we protect lesser folk than the President—you and me—from such a denial of our rights as Mr. Hoffman and his mini-legions are capable of denying us, in their quixotic but not altogether toothless campaign for revolution. The Jeffersonian ideal continues to be exemplary: the Hoffmans and the Dellingers and the Cleavers should be laughed, or disdained, into impotence.

Even so, there is a creeping difference between,

for instance, the way in which the whole of the American public reacted against the white racists who assaulted the civil rights advocates during the sixties, and the way in which the community reacts now to the disruptions of the New Left revolutionaries. Mr. Allard Lowenstein recently told me that it is not a new experience for him to be silenced, and even threatened and clubbed down, by those who disagree with him. But when he was given such treatment by Ku Klux-types in the South, in the early sixties, the whole of America reacted in horror and registered its solidarity with him and the others who worked for a continuing attrition of the birthmark that the Civil War did not altogether succeed in erasing. A few months ago, addressing a university audience at Columbia, Mr. Lowenstein was hooted down and literally silenced for defending the right of Professor Herman Kahn to speak unmolested, and faculty members in that audience countenanced and even egged on the Jacobinical furies that ruled the crowd—who needless to say went unpunished, even unreprimanded, although they most indisputably conspired together to abridge the civil liberties of two men, Herman Kahn and Al Lowenstein, who have never by word or deed disparaged the civil liberties of any American citizen.

PROPOSITION FOUR: *So far have the professionally tolerant gone towards fantacism that we stand in danger of losing the salutary force of public sanction.*

It is always least desirable to have to write new laws, or even to have to invoke laws that have be-

209

come flaccid from disuse. Consider a recent incident.

If it blurs in the mind just what and who are the Black Panthers, why they are an organization founded a few years ago on the doctrine that the United States is a racist-oppressive country best dealt with by the elimination of its leaders and institutions. Suggestive of its rhetorical style is the front page of its house organ which featured on the day after his death a photograph of Robert Kennedy lying in a pool of his own blood, his face transformed into the likeness of a pig.

Do you think Robert Kennedy was a pig? I asked Eldridge Cleaver a while ago. Yes, he said. Did Mr. Cleaver believe in the elimination of pigs? Yes, he did. Well, why not begin with Nixon; surely he is the chief pig? I observed. Mr. Cleaver, who has had intimate experiences with the law, advised me that he knew enough not to counsel directly the assassination of the President, but that if in fact someone did kill him, that would surely be one less pig in the world. Those who believe that Cleaver, and derivatively his followers among the Panthers, have mellowed may look at the introduction Cleaver wrote to Jerry Rubin's book, published last spring by the august house of Simon & Schuster—putting us in mind of Lenin's comment that when the last of the bourgeois is hanged, a capitalist will sell the hangman the rope—in which introduction Mr. Cleaver, an official of the Black Panthers, urges his disciples in America, black and white, to "rise up and kill pigs," and recalls as the most precious memory of his political experience in America a shoot-out in Oakland, California, at which he ob-

210

served that after one salvo, "a pig white lay dead, deep fried in the fat of his own bullshit."

Mr. Cleaver is not in this country, his career as visiting professor at Berkeley having been interrupted by a parole court. We cannot do anything about him.

So what do we do about the other Black Panthers, of which Mr. Cleaver is the spiritual leader? Well, that depends on who we are. If we are Leonard Bernstein, the conductor, we have a big cocktail party (a party about which Mr. Tom Wolfe has had absolutely the last say) to which we invite a local representative of the Panthers, and summon wealthy and artistic men and women, at which party money is raised for the Panther defense fund.

Mr. Bernstein was modishly dressed, in turtleneck sweater and double-breasted jacket, and had obviously been studying up on the idiom of the times; indeed so thorough is Mr. Bernstein that it is altogether possible that he staged a rehearsal or two, because a dialogue with a Black Panther is every bit as difficult to perform as, say, a symphony of Schönberg. Anyway, the Black Panther, Mr. Cox, began by announcing that if business didn't provide full employment, then the Panthers would simply take over the means of production and put them in the hands of the people, to which prescription it is recorded that Mr. Bernstein's reply was, "I dig absolutely."

Mr. Cox told the gathering how very pacific he and his confederates are, that ultimately of course they desire peace, but that they have been attacked in their homes and murdered in their beds and

211

have the right to defend themselves. "I agree one hundred per cent," Lenny said, neglecting to ask Mr. Cox to explain to what defensive uses his confederates intended to put the hand grenades and Molotov cocktails that were discovered in the raids.

I remember in the hour I spent with Mr. Cleaver the one thing I said to him that made him truly angry. It was that the Black Panther Party exists primarily for the satisfaction of white people, rather than black people. The white people like to strut their toleration, and strip themselves of their turtleneck sweaters to reveal their shame. The Panthers have only a few thousand black members, because the mass of the black people are too proud, too unaffected, to join the Panthers, to attend Leonard Bernstein's parties. Meanwhile, that party will serve, for a long time one hopes—I hope—as the symbol of total moral confusion; as a black mass on the altar of toleration. It suggests at the very least the failure of even aristocratic public opinion to rise to the responsibility of elementary moral distinctions.

PROPOSITION FIVE: *Although such as Eldridge Cleaver can be extremely specific ("kill the pigs"), the vagueness of the revolutionary program of much of the New Left is its most singular strength, confronting the republic with its subtlest extralegal challenge.*

It is a commonplace to observe that those of a rebellious spirit in our midst do not know what they want. And even that they do not know by what means to achieve the conditions they cannot

212

specify. I consider these data rather less reassuring than otherwise. If the revolutionists were committed to an identifiable program, they might be approached with demonstrations that their program, or any approximation of it, is not producing the goods (in Cuba, say, or in the Soviet Union). Curiously, the failures of Communism are more often treated as a joke than as a tragedy. (As in the current jollity: What would happen if the Communists occupied the Sahara? Answer: Nothing—for 50 years. Then there would be a shortage of sand.) But precisely the loose-jointedness of their mode—the de-ideologization of their movement—the disembodiment of the eschaton—leaves the revolutionists in a frame of mind at once romantic and diffuse, and the rest of us without the great weapon available to King Canute, who was able to contrive what would nowadays be called a Confrontation between—the ineluctable laws of nature and the superstitions of his subjects.

So that the idea of revolution continues to excite the political and moral imagination. It is necessary, in making one's complaints against the society we intend to replace, to be vague and even disjointed. To be specific, or to be orderly, is once again to run the risk of orderly confutation. General charges are not so easily denied; indeed they are not really deniable. How do you deny, for instance, the sweeping charge that "all of politics is the organization of greed"? "Misery abounds" is a descriptive phrase which could accurately be used about every society that was ever organized on the face of the earth.

What ails them? Or—if you prefer—us? I quote

213

now not from any of the better known advocates of revolution. I reach instead for a stretch of prose unencumbered by sophistication of thought or of style; what one might call the Volkswagen of revolutionary manifestos. Here it is, from a professor of political science at Hunter College in New York City, published in Volume I, Number 1 of a "revolutionary" journal.

The established system, he complains, "comprises elements of the archaic Judeo-Christian theocratic traditions,
elements of the dark-age autocracy,
feudalism,
militarism,
zoological capitalism [I am not quite sure what he means by that, but I have a feeling I am one],
corporate monopolism and plutocracy,
with an admixture of 19th century liberalism and trade union socialism."
Now there is no doubt that these are indeed some of the historical, cultural, and philosophical tributaries that flow into America. But hear what the professor says they have produced.
They have produced to begin with an *"antisocial orientation, based on the private profit motivations."* This in turn "produced most . . . of the evils of the present system. Among those evils are the following:
the transformation of man into an instrument of production,
an indiscriminate exploitation of natural and human resources,
the promotion of vulgarity,

214

an excessive consumption coexisting with poverty,
the scarcity of housing,
the pollution of air, water and food,
unemployment,
urban decay,
the reduction of woman to a sex symbol,
crime,
racial discrimination,
and the transformation of universities into an instrument of the military-industrial complex."

How can one argue with the man who holds America responsible for *all* the evils, *all* the ugliness, *all* the distractions we see, hear, and know about in America? It is not my purpose here to argue with the revolutionist the justice of his several indictments, or the merit of his "solutions." It is all very well to take the revolutionists by the scruff of the neck and show them that, as Professor Toynbee preaches, revolutions historically have not brought about the ends explicitly desired, but something very like their opposite; but the success of such demonstrations presupposes a clinical curiosity on the part of the observer, and such is not the temper of those in America who are talking about revolution. The point to stress is that the allure of revolution, and the importance of revolutionary attitudes in contemporary political and social affairs, are bound to grow, in the existing climate, not only because the sanctions of stability are not being pressed, but precisely because every modern aggravation—as we have just seen—is nowadays transformed into yet another cause for revolutionary commitment; and the ideologists of revolution are careful, as in the passages above, to tread a line enough on the specific side of generality to describe a recognizably American situation, yet far enough short of specificity to permit them constantly to nourish the revolutionary imagination—to stimulate the confidence that liberation lies just over there on the other side of the barricades, even as Nat Turner dreamed that if only he could make it to the Dismal Swamp, the world would begin anew.

There is very little hope in arguing with those who are attracted to the religion of revolution. James Baldwin, in his furious and moving polemic *The Fire Next Time*, argued that "the only thing the white people have that black people need, or should want, is power." Power, that great amulet. Power to do what? As one observer forlornly asks, in an essay on Stokely Carmichael, "What makes Stokely Carmichael think that the Negroes will use Power to better advantage than the whites have been able to use it? I know there is no great point in describing the disappointments of freedom to the untutored [man]. But Stokely Carmichael is a tutored [man]. He may hope that the Negro would master Power rather than be mastered by it, but his tutoring must have acquainted him with the dictum of Confucius: 'He who says, "Rich men are fools, but when I am rich I will not be a fool," is already a fool.' "

Nor is that difficulty unique to the black revolutionists. The critic Professor John Aldridge has said of the young white revolutionists that one

216

"become[s] aware of paradoxes and contradictions which suggest that their actions derive not from a coherent ideology or even a coherent emotional attitude but more nearly resemble a series of random gestures enacted in a climate of metaphysical confusion."

Professor Aldridge brings together a few of the relevant paradoxes and inconsistencies of the young revolutionists:

—"their preoccupation with style and their boundless appetite for banality";

—"their indifference to standards of personal conduct when applied to them by adults, and their insistence upon the most exemplary standards of conduct when applied by them *to* adults";

—"their obsession with the nature and quality of university instruction and their [lack of] interest in ideas, imaginative literature, and the values of the humanistic tradition";

—"their passion for individuality and their belief in collective action and [their practice of] group conformity";

—"their mystical belief in the primacy of intense feeling, the soul-rejuvenating benefits of fresh emotional experience, and their deep fear of uncertainty, contingency, and risk—all those situations of adventure and test which give the edge of fatality to life."

"Although"—Professor Aldridge concludes— "they have more freedom of action, feeling and opinion than any generation before them in our history, they are outraged by the existence of forces which in the slightest degree threaten to restrict or

217

program or manipulate their responses. Yet if their dream of a problem-free society could ever be realized, it would very likely be a society in which the full horror of IBM-card anonymity had descended, in which all human responses would be programmed, probably at birth, the last hope of individual freedom of distinction erased by technocratic egalitarianism, and misfits and rebels, the scruffy, unwashed, and bizarrely costumed, would most certainly be the first to perish under the sword."

So that reason is not availing, not in the current mood. Reason cannot reach the revolutionary vapors on which the men and women we speak of are stoned. What is required, I think, is among other things a premonitory Sign; let's not say what it is, but let's hope that the academic community will help in devising it, in making it firm, yes, but humane; such a sign as Hamilton foresaw might from time to time need to be shown. A sign that suggests a corporate reaffirmation of the community's ideals, the most pressing one being its decision to survive—all this keeping in mind the words of Belloc, who, observing the rise of Hitler in Europe, wrote:

"We sit by and watch the Barbarian, we tolerate him; in the long stretches of peace we are not afraid. We are tickled by his irreverence, his comic inversion of our old certitudes and our fixed creed refreshes us; we laugh. But as we laugh we are watched by large and awful faces from beyond; and on these faces there is no smile."

And so, unsmilingly, we face the requirements of the current situation; and these are that we stand

218

firm, and say No, our justification being that for all its faults, this is, and we pledge that it shall continue to be, a lovely country.

There now, Number 3. I wish Mr. Levine had sat through it.

The question period wasn't long, and wasn't particularly spirited. I had told my nephew that after it was over I would visit his freshman lodgings. Hunt is tall, handsome, courtly, and had the reputation at prep school of being the vaguest boy in the history of the world. In the months since graduating he has improved on the reputation. As a very little boy, blond, silent, unsmiling, appealing, he had been my father's favorite; and after my father's paralytic stroke, they spent very long hours together, happy in each other's silent company. Hunt was taken by his parents to live in Spain, where he acquired a slight Spanish accent which even now is detectable. I remember visiting him and my son, at Portsmouth, a few weeks into their freshman term. I knew he would have special difficulty getting used to English, after ten years in Spain, and I asked, How are you getting on? "Fine, Uncle Bill," he answered in his clipped tones. "Only I am having a little bit of trouble with orthography."

We arrived at Farnam Hall where eight or ten students were waiting for us. I looked about anxiously. No whiskey, no coffee, no beer, no Coca-Cola, no ginger ale, no cider, no pretzels; just Hunt, smiling his welcome. I made a choking sound. Oh, said Hunt; yes. He asks around, does anybody have anything to drink in his room? Everyone looks around inquiringly, one or two fan out into adjacent rooms, and from somewhere somebody

219

produces a bottle of Old Crow with a downtrodden jigger left in it. The bottle is ceremoniously handed to me by Hunt, in the glass he brings in from the bathroom, from which glass he has just now plucked his toothbrush, which he continues to hold in his hand, until one of his roommates casually lifts it from him, and deposits it on Hunt's bed, a mattress that lies, for reasons unexplained, across the floor of the same living room where we are gathered; which reasons, from a long knowledge of Hunt, I do not now probe.

After a while, after much social-philosophical badinage I said I was hungry and thirsty, and half a dozen of us went out to forage for refreshment. I suggested we go to the Fence Club, my old fraternity. I wanted, among other things, to greet the resident manager of it, a large, retiring, authoritative figure, who was there even before my brothers John and Jim became members. I had written him a note two years ago, on reading that his son had been killed in Los Angeles at a closed meeting of militant blacks; and, now, his widowed daughter-in-law is being tried, along with Bobby Seale, for complicity in the murder of Alex Rackley. But Fence was closed (at ten o'clock!); and so were the adjacent fraternities, which like Fence are far gone in desuetude, for reasons nobody entirely understands, though everybody agrees they have something to do with the affluence-cum-egalitarianism paradox. We walked on in search of what I now had crystallized as absolutely essential to my immediate well-being, namely a beer and a hamburger. Over there at a joint on Chapel Street you can buy sandwiches. It is called The Normandy . . . We used to refer to it as

Charley's, when I was at Yale, Charley being the owner-operator. We became very good friends, and when Charley was busy I used to punch the cash register myself and make my own change, until Charley's Greek brother-in-law, who was the cook and co-owner, flatly objected on the grounds that such an honor-system could easily be abused by others who, taking note of my habits, might insist on the same lackadaisical privileges. I remember Charley serving me the proscription shamefacedly, but he made up for it a few weeks later when he resolutely declined to press charges against the *Yale Daily News*, notwithstanding his brother-in-law's quite understandable insistence that he should do so in protest against the public impression, created by the *News*, that Charley's was a restaurant to go to if you wanted to be poisoned.

The tradition at the *News* is to get the "heelers" quite drunk before announcing to them, at the end of their grueling eight-week apprenticeship, which of their number have been elected to the Board. The ceremony reaches cyclical heights of debauchery every few years as the management struggles, asymptotically, towards the goal of fully anesthetizing the losers' pain; after which climaxes unsmiling deans tranquilize the next few celebrations, which however begin in due course to rise towards the old objectionable peaks, as the memory of the deans' warnings recedes. I remember when I was a first-term freshman, too junior yet to heel, walking leisurely down York Street late at night with a friend. Suddenly a young man, stark naked, ran rapidly by us from the opposite direction, followed at sprint-speed by another young man holding a raincoat in front of him, said raincoat obviously intended to overwhelm the nakedness of the young heeler, who in his exuberance (if indeed he had just learned of his election to the Board) had clearly gone too far; even as, in dejection (if he had *not* been elected), he had likewise gone too far. I was not altogether surprised to recognize the pursuing party, with the raincoat cocked, as my brother, the future senator from New York, who, because of the post-war scarcity of qualified *News* personnel, had volunteered his services as senior editor once-a-week, while studying at the Law School. This particular week his duties evidently involved (he was either the nearest man around at the party, or else the quickest on the draw, when the heeler stripped and bolted) clothing the nakedness of the heeler-gone-wild; and on they ran, closely followed by a posse of *News* personnel and policemen.

Two years later, another peak of irresponsibility. I was the chairman. We gave the heelers' party in my suite at Davenport College, and the Managing Editor, my former roommate Tom Guinzburg, exercising the traditional duties of his office mixed the drinks: which is easy enough to do if you merely dump, as Tom did for the 27 heelers (only 11 of them would be elected), 27 bottles of gin into a barrel, and then, ceremoniously (Tom is a purist), one bottle of Vermouth. After a half-hour of chug-a-lugging, a great raucous was born, and presently the telephone rang. The College Master—demanding the immediate evacuation of my quarters. I called Charley and asked him please instantly to prepare 54 hamburgers, which, unquestioning, he proceeded to do. Then I attempted to bring the elatedly distraught heelers to attention, so that

222

we might file out to Charley's, a block away. A cherubic 18-year-old finally volunteered to lead the procession, stepped outside my door, and collapsed astride the hallway, resplendently unrevivable, a plastic smile smeared over his angelic face. Bad enough under any circumstances, especially bad tonight because at that precise moment the weekly, full-dress Fellows' parade, issuing regally from the Master's Suite next door, routed inexorably down our corridor to the dining room below; and, perforce, the gentlemen had to pass, nay one by one had to step over, the corpse of our immobilized heeler, the personification of Innocence Traduced at Yale. I remember it was Thornton Wilder, as Senior Fellow, who had first to step over the body; he smiled urbanely at me and Tom, as if he had negotiated a mud-puddle. The Master's smile was less complaisant. We got to Charley's, and there, as if on signal, *all* 27 of the freshmen were sick; a few of them taking instant relief on Charley's counter, others—the chivalrous majority—rushing outside to the sidewalk, giving passersby, however, the indelible impression that Charley's was a ptomaine-poison-joint; which was the complaint that Charley's poor brother-in-law struggled to press, but which Charley grandly waived, on kids-will-be-kids grounds. Back at the *News*, Tom read out the election results to 24 comatose and three semi-conscious bodies, which the senior staff then wheelbarrowed to their rooms over the next two hours, the lucky ones (among them my brother Reid) not discovering until dawn their good fortune; the unlucky ones facing, the next day, the aggravated pain of paralyzing hangovers *and* rejection by the *News*. I thereupon modi-

223

fied the election party procedures, having endured a tongue-lashing from the College Master, which was okay; just so Charley wasn't sore at me . . .

Across the way from Charley's you can buy a beer, but there is no place in sight where you can do both—in a community of ten thousand students! So we sat down at a bar, and one of the boys went out and brought back hamburgers, and then we left to return to the *News* Building, where Jerry and Rowley were waiting. I said goodnight to my escorts, sank into the back seat, looking forward gratefully to Silence, and dutifully to the pile of manuscripts Priscilla has approved for *National Review*, on which my own decision is overdue. I am waving goodbye and the car begins to pull out, when one of the boys opens the door, and asks, "Mr. Buckley, are you driving to New York?" Yes, I said. "Can I ride with you?" One has to react immediately in such circumstances. The slightest hesitation is emotionally lethal. "Of course," I said; and move the papers and briefcases to make room for him, pressing the lever to raise the glass partition.

I recognize him from Hunt's party. He is eighteen or nineteen, blond, shy of manner. He begins to recount his misgivings about American society, the war, the draft, the profit system, the educational establishment. He is charming, and entirely sincere, but I am very nearly exhausted, and I wish that I had such staying power as Allard Lowenstein, who has never been known to take the initiative in terminating a conversation with any student. My answers are diffuse, banal, and repetitious; and then, passing Darien, I think to interrupt for long enough to ask where in New York City is he headed. He replies that in fact he is not headed anywhere, that if I will simply leave him any old place in Manhattan, he will go to Grand Central and take the next train back to New Haven. Great God, I said, is he aware that it is past midnight, and trains don't run after midnight to New Haven? No bother at all he says: absolutely none; he will sleep at Grand Central, and take any old morning train in plenty of time to get back to class. So I bop the lever and tell Jerry to drive to my house in Stamford.

I approach it warily because my beloved Eudosia, who is Cuban, very large, quite old, altogether superstitious, and speaks only a word or two of English (even though she has been with us for 19 years), is *quite* certain that the gentleman who raped the 16-year-old girl in New Caanan three years ago and escaped has successfully eluded the police only because of his resourceful determination to ravage Eudosia before he dies. Accordingly she demanded, and I gave her, a shotgun, into which I have inserted two empty shells. Still, Eudosia with blank cartridges is more formidable than Eugene McCarthy with The Bomb. Only a month ago a telephone repairman, achieving his DMZ astride a tree-top, was forced to tap the telephone line, so as to ring my sister Priscilla at the office in New York, to report that Eudosia was at ground level, shotgun cocked, and would Priscilla please call her to explain over the telephone in Spanish, the innocence of his intentions? I stop at my garage-study, and ring Eudosia on the house phone, announcing our approach; and she opens the door. I take Scott to my son's bedroom, fish out a fresh toothbrush from Pat's larder, leave word with Eudosia to please give him breakfast, and head on to New York.

225

Now, in the mail, a letter. He writes, "Dear Mr. Buckley: My first reaction to my own presumptuousness last night [a little wooden] should probably be a questioning of my own sanity [graceful]. I don't really know why I found it necessary to take advantage of your kindness in burdening you with my hang-ups; but I'm glad now that you accepted my company, and I think I profited greatly from our discussion [polite]. I guess all young people have some difficulty relating to the seemingly gigantic and inhuman American institutions, so sitting in the back seat of a car with someone whom I've always considered an institution in himself was, for me, an invaluable experience [as much could be said about sharing the back seat with a bald eagle]. Actually, I'm still having a bit of trouble realizing the reality of last night's experience—it seems like something out of a ridiculously romantic novel [charming]. Anyway, I'll always remember your kindness and understanding [perfunctory], and you will always have my respect [unguarded]—not only for being an intellectual institution, but also for being a friend. Thanks, [Dylan]."

I reply, "I like spontaneity, and yours was a wonderfully spontaneous thing to do, in particular since you did not know where you would be spending the night. I only regret that the awful fatigue [self-pitying] that overtakes me after a public performance [self-serving] left me unequal to the challenges you put to me. As an Institution, I have a great deal to learn. Anyway, I am sending you a copy of my recent book [*Did You Ever See a Dream Walking?*] which, if you will give it a chance, will do much better by you, I promise, than I was able to do riding between New Haven and Stamford. Come by any time. And if my nephew across the hall runs out of tooth-paste, think kindly of him."

I do not know exactly why, but there is no doubting that many students are attracted not so much to public figures (I speak about the opinion-mongers) whose principles are fixed, but to public figures who are willing to take exposed positions that logically extend from theoretical commitments, and, for the most part, in the polemical world, these are: the conservatives—who, accordingly, arouse a special curiosity.

Exactly a year earlier I encountered another student, less worldly by far than my Yale friend. I wrote about him, called him my ideological Pygmalion, even though the bright young editors in my office told me I should call him my "Galatea," reproaching me for making the Frank-enstein-error. No matter.

He is 19 years old, a second-year student at the University of Pittsburgh, all beard and beads from the chest up, and below that, scruffy gabardine. I cannot describe his face, never having penetrated the beard. He sat next to me one evening in the car that took me to the airport after my lecture, another student driving, three more in the back seat, one of them entirely blind, brandishing a tape-recorder and asking such questions as "What do you and your son talk about?" My Pygmalion was interested in grander themes. To say that he comes to politics with tabula rasa would cause the founding of a Tabulae Anti-Defamation League. My Pygmalion said things like, "Like, I jus' don't figure how you come and give a speech and say you're for Vietnam and collect your fee and then jus' go away, like man, you don't know what it means, you make war sound cool. I'm not going to

Vietnam and have my face blown off or my arms or something, why should I?" I looked at him and wondered (once again from the depths of a post-performance fatigue) just where to start, where to start. I tried the usual analysis. Look, I said, wars are not beloved of the warmakers, at least not as a general rule. Look, I said, wars are because there is something worse than wars, like life in Russia or in China or in North Vietnam. Look, I said, if you don't want to live in America because you think America is diseased and because America makes decisions that involve other people's heads and limbs being blown off, you can do lots of things about it, even including leave America. "If I'm going to split, I'm going to think about it first." I didn't say that that experience might prove more painful even than going to Vietnam. "I went to the Iron Curtain countries this summer," he said, "like even to Albania, and they weren't so bad. On th'other hand"—he speaks gently, like St. Francis to the birds—"I know they didn't show me what they didn't want to show me." He smiled.

We reached the airport in time to have a drink or a coffee before the flight. The others ordered a daiquiri or a whiskey sour or a beer, but Pygmalion ordered a Coke; he doesn't drink booze. At the gate he said he wanted to tell me "something private." I leaned over, and what he said was, "Look, if you want, I'll go on the plane with you to New York and you can explain all those things. Don't worry about the money; I'll use my student pass." No, I told him—abruptly I fear—it's too late at night. But I sensed that he felt the shock of rejection, so I said, Look, call me up tomorrow, here's my private telephone number. "When?" "Between two-thirty and three-thirty in the afternoon." I got to my office at two thirty-five. He had already called, and was told I wasn't in. He did not leave his number, or call again, and I knew he thought that I had put him on, like the military-industrial complex.

But a week went by and then his easy-soft voice came over, like he was coming to New York to work for Lindsay before the election, and would I visit with him? Of course. He got to the office a little early and slipped into my secretary's office wearing a weatherbeaten coat, which he took off and plopped smack in the middle of the floor, and then he leaned on the filing cases and made some gentle-talk. Miss Bronson gave him a book of mine and he slipped it between his back and his belt where, I suppose, it rested comfortably; and in due course he came in and we chatted. Mostly about marijuana, because it was on his mind. What's the matter with grass? Well, I said, nobody knows exactly, but just to take one specific thing, you can't tell if someone's had grass, but people who have, lose control and, for instance, they can run over kids while driving cars. Grass doesn't affect a driver's control, said my Pygmalion assertively. Yes, it does, I contradicted him, because I know a doctor who says so and who writes for the New York *Times,* and nobody who writes for the New York *Times and* is a doctor *doesn't* know what he's talking about, right? He smiled his shy smile, and I felt terribly inadequate. We went down to the street and drove off. I took him to the subway to catch his train to Brooklyn, where he was to poll-watch for John, and presently I received a letter from him: "Dear Mr. Buckley: During our discussion on pot you said something to the effect of one of the results

229

of legalizing pot would be an increase of auto accidents due to stoned drivers. I must confess that during the time we visited I was completely stoned. The reasons that I smoked pot before I came to see you were several and one was not because I thought it would be cool to see 'Mr. Buckley' from a stoned vantage point. But rather a) a complete stranger gave me a few joints, b) I was afraid to carry joints on my trip to see you, c) I met a groovy cop who wanted to turn on so naturally I turned on. I hope that during the time we met I conducted myself in a fitting manner (whatever that may have been) and if so I present proof that a person can control himself while being stoned. Therefore I hope I have dismissed your fears that legalizing pot will increase the rate of irresponsible acts committed by heads. Sincerely [signature]—I thank you most gratefully for meeting me."

I didn't hear from him again. Dylan, on the other hand, wants a summer job at *National Review*.

Enough. It is time for lunch. Pat hasn't been to Maxwell's Plum, and it is Peter Glenville's current enthusiasm, so we have agreed to go there. We set out, walking (the taxis are on strike) in the bitter-bright cold. Peter is always the (most engaging) conversationalist, and, chatting along, we trail behind Pat, who addresses the cold wind like a dogged serf, leaning against it silently, resignedly, her head muffled in a shawl, looking neither right nor left. There, at Maxwell's, is Rosalyn's painter-friend waiting for us, and we while away a contented hour in the crazy-attractive Victorian-modern stained-glass decor. Then we walk to Peter's, on 64th, to look at his New York *Times*, because we have decided to go to the movies, and to invite to join us Peter's friend Bill Smith.

Everyone is in favor of seeing a different movie, but we are limited by the taxi strike to what is close by, and finally decide—much against Pat's wishes because she-saw-*Woodstock*-and-hated-it—to see the documentary that opens today on the Altamont festival in California. I note sneakily that it is probably something I can do a column on; it is, and late tonight, in Washington, I write about it...

In case you didn't know it, the important event of 1969 in Kidworld was Altamont. Not because it was a spectacular, at which 300,000 young people came together to worship The Rolling Stones, but because someone was killed there.

You see it all in a movie just out which they choose to call *Gimme Shelter*—which, for all I know, means something in Kidspeak. Briefly, when the estimates came in (it was almost exactly a year ago, on December 6), The Stones faced the problem that the crowds descending onto the Altamont Speedway would rival and perhaps even exceed those that came together earlier in the year at Woodstock, N.Y. Everyone went into a whirl of activity to put together the essentials for such a gathering. Melvin Belli, the lawyer, seems to have accepted the role of coordinator and there are bits and pieces of him strewn throughout the picture. He talks into a telephone, and mysterious voices come in from various parts of the world, as the problems are touched upon: how to look after so many kids.

It isn't shown just when or why The Stones decided to use the services of Hell's Angels; but use them they did, and before long you see them there, arriving on their motorcycles, bearded (mostly), and beefy, Marlon Brando generation, looking old and jaded, as if they had spent too many years at one of Hitler's torture gardens to take much pleasure in routine sadism. The juxtaposition of the Angels of Hell and the Flower People stays in the memory.

Meanwhile The Stones themselves have arrived, by helicopter, and are shepherded into a trailer, whence from time to time Mick Jagger, who is the Chief Stone, emerges, to vouchsafe an autograph, to chat with the bodyguards, or merely to peer out at the brawly scene. Although there are extensive shots of the other Stones, Jagger is as much the center of attention as Bernadette would be in a movie about Lourdes. He is everywhere, and he is fascinating. Primarily he is fascinating because one simply does not know what it is that he *does* that is fascinating. He does not play a musical instrument. His voice couldn't be better than that of, say, every fourth person listed in the telephone directory. His features—and indeed those of the other Stones—are composed as if they were practicing to make it easy for David Levine to draw them: angular, unanimated, droopy in the philosophical rather than weary sense; homely. He is always heavily costumed, with preposterous pants and shoes, and usually a drape trailing down from each arm. He is in constant motion, and here the movements are electric. He strides all over the stage, head jostling, hips vibrating, hand-mike up close to his lips, howling away at songs that are apparently well known to everyone in the audience, which is transported with pleasure, while the drums go crazy, the guitars feel out their dissonances, in search (futile) of Oriental resolution. That's all; and to have one final look at him at the end of his American tour is what Altamont was all about.

So there the Angels were, to keep order. Their principal instrument of discipline is the billiard cue, with which they whack to the right of them, whack to the left of them, attempting to keep the kids away from the hastily constructed stage that was set up in the middle of Farmer Brown's spread, just out from San Francisco. It is mostly unavailing. The kids slurp up over the human barbed-wire, and it transpires in the consciousness that they are, at least a great many of them, stoned on drugs. Two or three times Mick is forced to stop the proceedings and plead with the audience to maintain a little order. "People!" he calls out. "People! Look, cool it! Come on now! Stop f——— this thing up! Otherwise we can't play. We *won't* play!" And then the direst threat. "We're going to *split!* Unless you cool it we're going to *split!*" And then a camera shot of yet another scuffle. Only this one has an air of finality to it and—flash forward—Jagger, viewing the rushes back in London, solemnly orders the director to run it again in slow motion. Because this is the scene in which one of the guardians of the stage, addressing a tall, slim, hopped-up Negro, brings down a knife, twice, into his back, and kicks him when he is down, and the Negro is dead. The Stones play on for a few minutes, and then they crowd, tightly, like members of their own audiences, into the helicopter, and fly out of the lonely crowd, leaving behind them the corpse of Woodstock Nation.

We walk back to 73rd, the senses jaded by the music and the noise, the beatings and the killing. Peter, Bill Smith, and I walk on to St. Jean's at 76th Street to hear Mass. The church is very nearly full, and I am reminded, as I am every Sunday, of what an aesthetic ordeal it has become, going to Mass, ever since the advent of the new liturgy: the dread vernacular, the conscripted congregational responses—to think that the architects of this profanation claim to have done it *for us!* At sermon time the priest announces that he will read a letter from Cardinal Cooke, which is being read at all Masses in New York City today. It is a flat condemnation of abortion, done through the device of a "diary" recorded by a fetus, which begins by chatting happily about its prospective entry into this world, then chokes off as it encounters the abortionist's knife. The dramatic narrative is followed by an unadorned homiletic. It is the most emphatic denunciation of abortion I have heard, and I suspect I had something to do with its promulgation because a few weeks ago I wrote a column on the subject: "It has greatly surprised many non-Catholics, and for that matter not a few Catholics, with what ease the abortionists have succeeded in making their permissive laws . . . which permit, let's face it, abortion-on-demand. It not only *seems* only yesterday, in fact it *was* only yesterday, that the accepted idea was that the Catholic political lobby made it impossible to permit the sale of contraceptives. To have proposed abortions ad libitum was, quite simply, unthinkable for a politician."

I offered as an explanation for the dispersal of this lobby the latitudinarian effect of Vatican II's statements on pluralism, which was succeeded by "the strange indecision that is the condition of the Church ever since . . . When [in America] the time came to rally protests against permissive abortion bills, the troops were simply not there. It is very difficult for a Catholic fundamentalist to go on about abortion being tantamount to murder, while his Cardinal is photographed speaking amiably to the leader of the Assembly that passed the abortion bill a few months before. Catholic voters are confused. Their bishops and their priests are complacent, or if that is not the word for it, they are undecided about what ought to be the rights of others, in pluralistic situations." I learned later that the Cardinal was startled by the column, and for reasons I did not intend. When I wrote that he had been "photographed" with the leader of the New York Assembly that passed the abortion bill, I had in mind the receiving line of the annual Al Smith Dinner in New York City, at which the Cardinal is the host, and which national and state leaders regularly attend. I was not present at the most recent of these dinners, but I had been to enough of them to know the procedure; to know that almost certainly the leader of the Assembly was there, and that almost certainly he was photographed—as is every luminary—on passing through the receiving line. Evidently it was as I had surmised. The leader of the Assembly had indeed been photographed with the Cardinal (though it was at a subsequent function), who interpreted my column as a personal reproach for having permitted such a picture; which reproach I had not intended: How *can* a cardinal host a dinner as straightforwardly ecumenical as this one (the proceeds of the dinner go equally to Jewish and Christian charities), and decline to shake the hands of the elected leader of the New York State Assembly? The social problem frames the political problem exactly: if abortion is murder pure and simple, then those who directly expedite murder do not qualify as guests at cardinals' functions. Surely, as John Noonan points out, even Catholics must begin to use a word different from "murder," even as we use an assortment of words to distinguish between, say, what an assassin does to his victim, and what a drunken driver does to his.

On this point I have become estranged from Brent Bozell, who founded a few years ago *Triumph* magazine, an organ of militant Catholicism which has elided now into an organ of militant anti-Americanism, reflecting the evolving intractability of its editor and his associates. The whole subject weighs heavily, and for once I find Catholics to the right of me, notwithstanding my own conviction that abortion is gravely, tragically, wrong.

. . . During the summer the editors of *Triumph* organized an institute in Spain that held sessions over a fortnight which several dozen Americans of various ages attended. I read about the organization of the institute, but did not know the character of it; until, this past week, I had a letter, of striking literary ability, from a young participant who described the lengths to which a few dispirited American Catholics are driven . . .

> I can only say it was grim, like the prose in *Triumph*—where every phrase is a funeral. And I don't mean that to sound invidious. Just descriptive of their journalistic mode, the rhetorical ambiance of those who see the enemy everywhere. Any outfit of Americans at sword's point with America will proceed with a certain grimness. And *Triumph* is, I most forlornly believe, as hostile to the American ethos as any revolutionary organ on the hard Left.
>
> Now, Mr. Buckley, I didn't know this until after we reached Spain. I'm so dumb. I knew they were deeply orthodox, literate, activist Catholics. At that I rejoiced. Moreover, I even glimpsed, without flinching, a few dark intimations about the horrific character of our age and society. Nothing unseemly there. After all, it is the business of The Church to despise

always the spirit of the age and I'm no Rotarian, so why shouldn't things dangerously wrong with America be found, photographed and denounced? Your magazine has been doing it for years. Now we have Nixon. Not enough I know, but the indices improve. Your brother was just elected. (Quick obiter: at one melancholy conversation with an editor I sat transfixed as he poured out this achingly eloquent lament about the desert that was America and how soon the blood of Christian Martyrs would be needed to nourish the cactus. Well, I suggested, snapping the spell, [we have] an oasis or two already; and argued that any system amenable to James Buckley's possible elevation into the Senate was not ready for the scrap heap. He smiled, then continued his dirge. It was depressing.) Of course, what I didn't know was the extent to which the Institute people viewed such evils as do surface and spread, as being organic expressions of a heritage perniciously anti-christian. That was offputting news.

I even remember the moment, or rather provocation, when the warheads were fired. It was early into the first week, scorchingly hot, and a few of us were in the bar sipping beer and exchanging backgrounds. Somehow the Jesuits got conscripted as a conversation-piece and everyone allowed as to how wicked they were. I demurred. And as I opined modestly about their great learning, offering John Courtney Murray as Exhibit A, I felt the coldest fury since my last skirmish with a liberal, months before. I quite expected an auto-da-fé in the courtyard followed by interment in the Escorial cellar. Of

237

course, the results were well short of ignominy. We had another beer and the talk turned to trifles. But that one scene managed to adumbrate a pattern of diatribe that would end only when we flew out in late August. I soon learned of other finks whose thought was proscribed. Willmoore Kendall, for instance. His sin? Why, naïvely supposing his countrymen decent and their nation's patrimony properly christian and constitutional. It is a myopia that soon afflicts all ex-residents of Idabel, Oklahoma [Professor Kendall's birthplace], who grow up believing the one is a synecdoche for the other and then get seduced into seeing the Federalist Papers as a tract other than the one Ayn Rand would write in order to glorify private greed.

And then, of course, pluralism was branded a fraud (I don't think more than four people had read *We Hold These Truths* [Father Murray's celebrated book], and those that did probably could not surmount their a priori hostility towards pluralism or Jesuits to plumb his argument); anti-communism an evil so long as atom bombs are stockpiled as retaliatory muscle, without which who would ever travel to Spain in order to denounce? Indeed the whole Conservative Movement was skewered day after dreary day. By late Aug. the debunking had reached a new level (one of tedium) when [one of] Mr. Bozell's eager epigone flew in to profane the Constitution. But unlike Bozell and [Professor Frederick] Wilhelmsen, whose minds really are magnificent (as metaphysician the latter is almost without peer—I only wish he'd work more at St. Thomas than Torquemada), this fellow did the job so clumsily that even ardent iconoclasts were dismayed. Short-lived I'm afraid. However, there were very few switcheroos. The gang that flew out was almost as motley as the one that flew in. The party line could never inspire categorical support. Not even on the issue of dogmatic fidelity to The Church, since we had non-catholics and even, God forbid, one or two agnostics. There was political heterodoxy as well. The Birchite mentality was in evidence. I must say very quickly however, that virulent bigotry was only the work of one or two. But as far as I know these few were never rebuked or their moral idiocies officially rejected i.e. in the way America was rejected. Nevertheless, I can see their abstract point. It is redundant to come out specifically against, say, antisemitism when the whole thrust of your apologetic is The Church Thing, as Chesterton would say. Still, it would have been good to hear. Like so many other things. . . . But before I close I do want to make clear this much. Notwithstanding those troubling summer days it was never time wasted. I learned an incredible amount, not the least of which was a profounder confidence in *National Review* . . .''

We walked back from church. Pat has prepared sandwiches and iced a bottle of champagne. Peter and Bill and I continue discussing the abortion question. Peter's first movie was *The Prisoner* starring Alec Guinness, a portrayal of the tribulation of Cardinal Mindszenty who was tortured by the Hungarian Communists in 1949 and force-fed through a show trial, in the fashion of Stalin-in-stride. Alec Guinness, absorbed by the experience, turned to Catholicism—he Poped, as they say in England

—and Peter was his godfather, except that if the convert is over twenty-one years old you use the term "sponsor," even as I was the sponsor of Brent Bozell, who joined the Catholic Church during our sophomore year at Yale. Peter's orthodoxy, even commingled with my own, leaves us incompetent to answer self-assuredly the question: What is the proper role of the dissenting minority in a pluralist society when it finds itself face to face with laws that permit what in church a few minutes earlier we had heard described *tout court* as murder? Granted that the frame of the Cardinal's letter was melodramatic, and that melodrama is inhospitable to distinction: even so—call it feticide and calliper as you will the differences exquisite between feticide and murder on the moral scale— what in fact do you *do*? I try out on Peter the arguments as distilled by Clare Boothe Luce in a manuscript I read earlier this week, which we will publish in *National Review* in January under the heading "A Catholic Looks at Abortion and the Pluralist Society." Clare, I tell Peter, having reviewed closely the works on abortion by Daniel Callahan and John Noonan, makes most penetratingly the point that the definition of "killing," notwithstanding the categorical, Mosaic proscription, has throughout post-Biblical history been explained politically. It has been (by and large) the civil authority that has distinguished between illicit, semi-licit, extenuated, and licit killing, ranging from first degree murder to war-making, with so very many shades in between, among them negligent homicide, the cuckold's dispensation, self-defense— the lot. Now the question is raised, by opportunistic advocates of abortion: Whence the *authority* of the *political "authority"* to deny the *authority* of the mother: and that, I think, is a constitutional-political sequence that needs to be confronted—or is it as simple (I incline to the opinion that it is) as that the mother, while obviously she exercises de facto authority over the survival of the fetus, is nevertheless legally, and a fortiori morally, nothing more than the custodian of the fetus whose insulation against abuse ought to be guaranteed by the state, to the extent—granted—that the state can ever serve successfully as a superintending custodian? This is *Question No. 1*, I insist to Peter; *Question No. 2* being: Which, in the range of available responses by Catholic and non-Catholic anti-abortionists, is the appropriate response? They range, hypothetically, from: a forthrightly mutinous relationship between the dissenter and the state, such as we are generally encouraged to believe was appropriate—indeed, ideally, imperative—between the German citizen and the Nazi government; and, at the other, placid extreme, mere rhetorical dissent. The range is wide. For instance, any anti-abortionist might categorically refuse to vote for any legislator who had given his sanction to permissive abortion laws. There are many permutations, including, as we approach the drastic, a total boycott of the civil processes. And so on. I insist to Peter, and he agrees, that on such questions Catholics-at-large necessarily depend on the formal leadership of the magisterium. If Cardinal Cooke wishes to inform us—in such unambiguous accents as for instance were used by Pius XII against the Communists in Italy before the crucial election of 1948—that no quarter can be given, that excommunication will inevitably apprehend the Catholic who voted for an abortion-licenser, then—then *let the Cardinal so inform us*. Is it appropriate for the individual Catholic, morally incensed, to prod the Pope towards moral rectitude? History adduces now and again a morally languorous pope who was awakened from his slumbers (and many more popes who slept through it all) by morally energetic laymen, preferably saints. Is this the current condition? Peter acknowledges the problem, Pat reminds us that the hour is late.

At exactly 10 P.M., which is not on Dr. Frank Stanton's clock to be confused with 10:05 P.M., his CBS jet will leave the Marine Terminal, with or without Pat and me aboard. Tomorrow Frank Stanton will preside over the monthly meeting of the United States Advisory Commission on Information, and Pat is joining me on this trip because tomorrow night Frank Shakespeare, the director of USIA, will give a formal (a *very* formal) dinner party at the State Department's dressy quarters, in honor of Stanton and me, who are the surviving members of the old Commission (to which Mr. Nixon will, after meeting with us at noon, announce the appointment of three new members), and the ladies in Frank's party are invited.

We eat, and whisk up the luggage—an inadequate way of describing what one does to accommodate Pat when she is poised to move from one city to another—and then, without Rowley, who is restrained in the hall, we step into the car, having said good night to Peter, who is off to Rome to vet the arrangements for *Man of La Mancha*, the movie version of which he has tentatively agreed to direct; and we slide out towards LaGuardia. Frank Stanton is there—courtly, authoritative, warm—and the two pilots. Frank fetches us up a drink even before we take off in the luxurious Gulfstream, with the wide, wide windows that give us a view of New York on an eye-stopping night, clear as the Arctic air, with here and there sheepish little aggregations of clouds hovering above the ground at a few thousand feet, as if furnished by CBS to give verisimilitude to the flight, which would otherwise be like one of those hygienic fancies one passes through at a New York World's Fair, at the General Motors exhibit. Pat is greatly taken by the plane, advising Frank that his hospitality would be complete if he could manage to devise a formula by which such an airplane might be put permanently at my disposal whenever I travel—or, in any case, whenever I travel with Pat. I begin to shake loose from them when Pat is demanding that Frank instruct her in the use of the telephone she spots at the side of the mini-lounge where she and he are seated, and Frank undertakes gallantly to engineer a call to whatever person she designates. I attempt to restrain her, arguing that the short trip will be utterly consumed with DO-YOU-READ-ME'S? OVER-AND-OUT'S. Then I impulsively abandon my role as Frank's protector against the dizzy-blonde who wants to press every stop in the brand-new organ, and go to an easy-chair, forward, to read again Herbert's letter, which I had not coped with the other day.

Herbert's reaction to the speech in Maryland, from his position on the left, is strangely harmonious with that of the young historian. He begins by thanking me for the lunch and apologizing for the few days' delay in writing, but says he is grateful that he did wait because he now has seen last Sunday's *Firing Line*, which was taped in London, the day before the debate with Galbraith, with three correspondents from the *Manchester Guardian* . . . "Your speech at Maryland, even though it was probably not the best that you ever gave, was the most brilliant I have ever heard, employing numerous logical and psychological devices to utter perfection. I came away very frustrated that evening; not because I had to stand down-stairs and listen over the intercom, but because I knew you were wrong but couldn't quite discover how, at least not until after considerable thought.

"When you mentioned that you take your morality from the Catholic Church and that that was why, princi-pally, you were opposed to abortion, I could not reply, within the confines of my thoughts, and find what pre-cisely was wrong with that statement. Now I know. Cer-tainly all people go through the same process as you. Dr. Wallace Culver, one of my mentors and an expert on the authoritarian personality and its relationship to religion, told me long ago that all people search for and accept or reject outside sources for their moral code. Some people accept a single source, this is one of the prime character-istics of authoritarianism, and others compile many varied experiences and sources. The process [you em-ploy] is very much the same [as mine] except *you* defer to the judgment and supposed revelations of the Catholic Church and its thinkers, while I go to other sources, Thomas Paine, Ingersoll, etc.

"You have a bad habit of combining one non sequitur after another, in such a rapid manner that they often go unnoticed. At Maryland I heard several non sequiturs that I do not recall at present . . . [Herbert nonetheless recalls one, in which the Black Panthers are the benefi-ciary]. In closing I would simply like to say that I deeply envy your superb talent. I hope that some day I shall possess similar abilities. Unlike you, I shall use those abilities for the good of people. Non sequitur."

But he is by no means through with me. "I thought your program Sunday night was the best you have ever

244

done and I would greatly like to see many more with similar format [the guests questioning me]. You handled yourself magnificently, so much so that you made one error after another and got away with it. This should be no reflection upon your three opponents as you move so quickly that it is only after careful deliberation that one realizes one has been snookered. A case in point . . . [in which the English, by contrast with the Americans, are the beneficiaries]. America wished to see the preservation of England from German rule only insofar as it would serve America's intentions.

"You also mentioned America's role in keeping the 'barbarians' at bay. One supposes that this must include the barbarian savages with which this continent was infested when Europeans first set foot upon it and the numerous barbarians of Africa that were later to populate the continent. Another one of your non sequiturs emerges, to wit, that barbarianism is a quality 'subsumed into the genus' Soviet or socialist—and certainly never American or capitalist—a very ingenuous assumption. A question arises: is it 'barbarian' to sit about weaving baskets and hunting with arrows—or would a more precise definition of the term include what occurred at Sand Creek, during the Chivington-Black Kettle massacre? [I confess that I am, until I reach the encyclopaedia, unfamiliar with the event.] To be sure, barbarianism no longer means, or is equated with, primitive technology, but rather with cruel and inhuman behavior of which we, as Americans, are equally as guilty as the Soviets. There is nothing in our historical experience, that I have ever run across, that would suggest that capitalism has any more restraining an influence upon human excess

245

than socialism or communism. [A lengthy passage follows, in which the architects of our Vietnam policies are the victims.]

"Another error I believe you committed was when you implied strongly that everyone has equal freedom of expression in this country when indeed they do not. To be sure, all varieties of thought are present; but it becomes a question of degree. Allow me to expand that concept. Whether or not a Panther can go out on the corner and sell his newspaper is not disputed. However, you will not disagree, your philosophy has a wider distribution than does Robert De Pugh's [Robert De Pugh is the chief figure in the crazy-right Minuteman movement], not due to any inborn truth in your ideas, for ideas are not born true but rather proven, but due to [your ideas'] greater degree of respectability. So, extreme opinions *can* be found in America, but if you are respectable, or at least acceptable to large numbers of Americans, you will naturally have, do I dare say so, MORE freedom of expression. To be sure, among the general population Hubert Humphrey has greater exposure than, say, the late George Lincoln Rockwell. Also, there are occasions when freedom of expression for extreme ideologies is absent. A case in point is police harassment of radical groups, particularly the Black Panthers and, I suppose it can be argued, Panther harassment of police. To the extent that such harassment does occur, there is a proportional decrease in the harassed groups' freedom. I recently witnessed police officers in Silver Spring, Md., arrest a Black Panther who was distributing the Panther newspaper on the corner of Colesville and Fenton Streets. It so happened that I went to school with one of the officers (I never use the term 'pig' as it sets fire to reason and has the same characteristics as the term 'nigger,' which is probably the single most destructive word in the English language), and played in a band with the other. Some days later I had occasion to speak with them about the arrest and I conducted myself in such a way as to lead them to believe that I was in complete agreement with their treatment of the Panther. It came out that they were told to arrest the 'fucking nigger' under any pretext just so long as he was off the sidewalk, 'not causing any trouble.' Now, of course, it does not matter one jot whether you agree or disagree with a man; you must, in a free society, accord him the same rights and freedoms that you accord yourself. To do otherwise is, to paraphrase Thomas Paine, to make a slave of yourself to your present opinion because you preclude yourself the right to change it. A society that allows freedom only to those individuals and ideas which it already accepts as truth is not a free society. The real proof of a free society is that society which not only tolerates diverse opinions and the expression of them, but is genuinely appreciative of their existence. As Walter Lippmann once said, we all have an obligation not merely to begrudgingly tolerate other opinions but to accept them with open arms and gratefulness, for it is these opinions that should be a free country's showcase. I will make no speculation as to the extent of police harassment of radical groups. I deem it sufficient to simply say, to the extent that it exists, there is a corresponding diminution of freedom in America. Point having been made, I won't bore you any longer."

Thus far what has Herbert given us? A sincere and moving effort to put forward a very familiar philosophical position. Notwithstanding the manifest callousness of the presentation, it is by no means naïve; sure, William

Douglas could do it better, but he would be saying essentially the same thing, in the enduring effort to harness America to the epistemological skepticism of Mill, and Holmes, and Dewey—and Ramsey Clark. Here is an exquisite demonstration, in fact, of where the implacable logic of relativism can take you: Herbert finds no grounds for significantly distinguishing between the historical performance of the United States and that of the Soviet Union. No more can Noam Chomsky. So much for Robert Conquest. So much for the crushing historical rebuttal of the defeated rationalism of Mill. But then, having flapped his wings in the sludge of a century's ideological effronteries, Herbert rises, to speak out in flute-tones, achieving a pure innocence, and authority; and from the heights he attains, he spots me, a speck on the landscape, and I am his victim, defenseless.

"I have written this lengthy diatribe in the hope that I might set some long-forgotten principle ringing in your mind. I feel that you are probably facing a problem that I am just beginning to face to a lesser degree; to wit, mental stagnation. I once knew a golden period when I believed that the greatest of all possible virtues that could be conferred upon a person was an open mind. I still believe that, but I am beginning to practice it less and less. I entered the educational experience with many deeply held misconceptions and it took me long to shake them off and it was not always a pleasant experience. Now I am again resisting change as I once did. I think you do much the same thing. Having expressed your beliefs so articulately and so strenuously for such a long time, you have become intellectually as rigid and inanimate [*inanimate!*] as those Soviet impolicy-makers you constantly inveigh against. You are a symbol, and, so the legend goes, symbols never change. Conservatism in America, in my opinion, owes everything to your efforts alone. If ever a movement depended for its continued growth upon the energy and boundless dynamism of one [*inanimate?*] man, constructive conservatism's dependence upon you is it. But meditate upon this: what will be your thoughts if when you come to your deathbed you look back and realize that all your life amounted to no more than one big highly successful game of power and self-glorification? I would never mention this or be so bold as to suppose that I, Mr. Ordinary, could offer you, William F. Buckley, any usable advice; but I have perceived the tendency in myself to play at games and have observed many of the same characteristics in you, and, since it can make a life so meaningless, I thought I might just offer my thoughts, with the best of intentions, that you may nod in agreement and maybe get something out of them. My biggest fear is that you will not read this letter, or dismiss it as cute. I hope not."

One wishes for the powers of John Henry Newman. But assuming that one possessed them, are the certitudes worthy? The certitudes of a middle-aged mid-twentieth-century American conservative? John Kenneth Galbraith, who is my friend, has approached me—Forgive my presumption, he begins, and I forswear the equal-and-opposite-reaction that the laws of mechanics and of debate prescribe—and I listen . . . *Give it up,* he says, seated next to me in the Volkswagen, as we head out from Gstaad towards the Rinderberg, which is where I like most to ski. *The whole thing.* National Review, *journal-*

ism, *television, radio, lecturing.* Come to the academy, and write *books.* It is only *books* that count. *I* did it. I left *Fortune,* and went to Harvard. The break must be absolute. You will need the *trauma.* Then—only then—you will discover the means to give a theoretical depth to your ideological positions.

But—I answer, in hindsight—the theoretical depth is *there,* and if I have not myself dug deeper the foundations of American conservatism, at least I have advertised their profundity. How can I hope to do better against positivism than Voegelin has done? Improve on Oakeshott's analysis of rationalism? (How does one illuminate a sunburst?) Rediscover orthodoxy more engrossingly than Chesterton did? What does it take to *satisfy,* to satisfy *truly, wholly?* More than Herbert's open mind, much more. More than Galbraith's theoretical depth. A sense of social usefulness . . . Herbert is hauntingly right—*c'est que la vérité qui blesse*—what are my *reserves?* How will I satisfy them, who listen to me today, *tomorrow?* Hell, how will I satisfy *myself* tomorrow, satisfying myself so imperfectly, which is not to say insufficiently, today; at cruising speed?

Frank Stanton's car is there, and the bags (of course) materialize, and he drops us by at the Hay-Adams, where Pat's sister is waiting for us, in from Pasadena for a Red Cross meeting, always for me and others a source of joy and stability. We chat noisily, for an hour, and then I retreat to a corner of the living room, to write my column on Altamont, which is due in New York in the morning, so I'll have to ask Miss Fahl, at the Commission, to phone it in tomorrow; early, so Harry won't be nervous.

Index

253

254

255